THE SECOND EPISTLE
TO THE CORINTHIANS

KARL SCHELKLE

CROSSROAD · NEW YORK

1981
The Crossroad Publishing Company
575 Lexington Avenue, New York, NY 10022

Originally published as *Der zweite Brief an die Korinther*
© 1964 by Patmos-Verlag
from the series *Geistliche Schriftlesung*
edited by Wolfgang Trilling
with Karl Hermann Schelke and Heinz Schürmann

English translation © 1969 by Burns & Oates, Limited, London
Translated by Kevin Smyth

Library of Congress Catalog Card Number: 81-68181
ISBN: 0-8245-0123-3

PREFACE

The problems of the relations between the two epistles to the Corinthians are numerous and complex, and they cannot be entirely passed over by one who desires a serious understanding of the epistles. The basic problems are briefly and clearly handled in the author's introduction, which should be read carefully. The reader will recognize that Second Corinthians is almost certainly assembled from more than one letter of Paul, and that the letters were written in a highly personal tone in response to a situation which is almost entirely unknown to us. When these problems are enumerated, it seems remarkable that Second Corinthians is as intelligible as it turns out to be.

The central problem of the interpretation of the epistle is the disruption of good relations between Paul and the members of the church of Corinth—more accurately, some of the members, and probably a minority. The proper relation of one Christian to another is Christian love; this love was threatened seriously. The letter makes it clear that some of the Corinthians had no respect for Paul as a person or as an apostle; and the last chapters of the epistle, which may be most or all of a separate epistle, are a sharp rebuke addressed by Paul to those who challenged his commission. There is no real parallel to this situation in the other New Testament books. A passage in Matthew 18 : 15–20, not paralleled in the other gospels, deals with the reconciliation of disputes, and faces the possibility that one of the parties may refuse to be reconciled. We have no information about any other problem similar to the problem of Paul and the Corinthians, and it seems altogether likely that there was no precedent for a dispute of this kind.

It was, therefore, incumbent upon Paul to set the standards of Christian love; he could not as an apostle wait for the Corinthians to arrive at a Christian position. He recognized his duty to make the first move towards reconciliation. But he encountered, perhaps for the first time in the Christian dispensation, the problem of reconciliation without the surrender of essential principles. The problem recurs frequently enough to make the study of Second Corinthians of some importance for Christian moral judgments. Fortunately this aspect of the problem can be grasped without detailed knowledge of the situation.

The essential principle which Paul was obliged to safeguard was the authority of the apostle. It must be understood from the beginning that it was not the mind of Paul or the mind of Jesus that Christian love should be sacrificed in favor of any other principle. If love is sacrificed, one is no longer speaking or acting in Christian terms. The problem arises because apostolic authority is itself an exercise of Christian love; and the apostle is not free to show his Christian love by the renunciation of his apostolic authority. But he is not free to vindicate his authority by the denial of love. The recalcitrant Corinthians had made it impossible, or attempted to make it impossible, for Paul to exhibit love by the exercise of authority.

His task, then, was to make his authority acceptable, not to impose it with no reference to the consent of those over whom it was exercised. Unless Paul could win their consent, his authority would cease to be Christian. Christian authority is by definition an authority which elicits the response of love by demonstrating love. Paul could have compromised his authority by yielding to pique. He could have compromised it by a kind of overbearing which would be understood in the exercise of civil or military authority. But Christian authority is not maintained by alienating those to whom it is directed. The possibility of a breach is real, but it is not the office of authority to open the breach.

Paul could accomplish his task because he did not let it become a question of personal dignity. Church unity and church authority were greater than the personal dignity of Paul; if anything could be readily and quickly sacrificed for unity and authority, it was the personal dignity and personal feelings of Paul. He was much more concerned with the personal dignity and personal feelings of the Corinthians, perhaps more than we might think he ought to be. But consideration for the dignity and the feelings of those with whom we have a difference is an indispensable prerequisite for reconciliation. The Corinthians could do without Paul, they could not do without the gospel and the church.

Certainly the words of Paul himself show clearly his own doubts as to whether he had overstepped the bounds of Christian tolerance and forgiveness, whether he had not given too much thought to his own person, whether he had not failed to distinguish between the vindication of apostolic authority and the vindication of the offended personal dignity of Paul. Such doubts, we have to say, are rare in disputes between Christians, as it is rare for Christians in similar situations to weigh the factors as scrupulously as Paul did. It is part of the apostolic mission to endure suffering, for through suffering the apostle shares in the redeeming suffering of Christ. It is not part of the apostolic mission to inflict suffering on others, but rather to spare them; and Paul was deeply concerned because he had caused pain.

Some comment such as the above seems altogether proper for the first nine chapters; it is not so obviously applicable to the last four chapters, in which the language of Paul is much more aggressive than it is in the first nine. It is this part of the epistle which is generally thought to form part of another epistle, and to cast some doubt on the beautiful image of Paul the reconciler; for in these chapters Paul hits hard, and it would be dishonest to pretend that he does not. But it is most probable that it is such language as the language of chapters 10–13 which caused the doubts and anguish which he expressed in chapters 1–9.

Let it be noted that Paul was here concerned with those whom he calls false apostles (11:13). Whatever the complaints were, they were of a character to cast doubt on Paul's apostolic authority and on the authenticity of the gospel which he preached. Paul shows no sign of a desire for reconciliation with the false apostles. The question was not whether Paul had to respond to such charges or insinuations, but what terms he should use in responding to them. The terms we read are harsh. When we read them, we must remember that we are overhearing a dialogue of which much is lost. Many conversations would sound quite hostile if they were heard detached from their context and their situation in life.

Even if this excuse be granted Paul, it appears that he found no perfect solution of his problem in personal relations, and that he himself was not satisfied with the solution. The value of his experience for us is not in an example which can be imitated in all details, but in the clarity with which the principles of the solution were perceived. The application of these principles to a concrete situation is quite another matter. If Christians fail in their application no more than Paul failed, they would do much better than they do. The evident bias of Paul towards tolerant and forgiving love is evident even in chapters 10–13, although it is not as clear as it is in chapters 1–9. It is almost impossible to maintain a clear head when one is personally and deeply involved in a problem, and it is a vain pretense to seek it. What the Christian can maintain instead of a clear head is a bias towards tolerant and forgiving love. He can remember that unity is more important than his personal feelings, and that authority maintained at the expense of love is really destroyed.

JOHN L. McKENZIE, S.J.

INTRODUCTION

The Apostle and His Office

It was probably in the spring of A.D. 50—the chronology of the life of St. Paul can be established only approximately—that St. Paul left Jerusalem for his second missionary journey. It took him first through Asia Minor, where he visited some of the churches founded during his first missionary journey. After a dream in which he saw a Macedonian appealing to him to come, he took the bold step of crossing over to Europe (Acts 15:36—16:10), preached first in Philippi and Thessalonica (Acts 16:11—17:19), and then traveled on to Athens and after that to Corinth (Acts 17:10—18:17). He says of the journey to Corinth: " I came to you in weakness and much fear and trembling " (1 Cor. 2:3).

St. Paul came in weakness. He was a sick man, burdened with bodily ills (12:7). He was poor and without means. He believed that he was bound to earn his living by his own hands, so as to be a burden to no one (11:7-11). He was therefore glad when he found Aquila and his wife Priscilla in Corinth, because he could carry on his trade as tentmaker in their workshop (Acts 18:2f.). He was also burdened by his anxiety for all the communities which he had founded, and which were still so much in need of his help. Unable to stay with all of them, the most he could do was try to help them through his letters and messengers (11:28). And he arrived in Corinth in fear and trembling. He had had very little success in Athens (Acts 17:24). Would the gospel gain a hearing in Corinth? Corinth was the capital of the Roman province of Achaia, and so the headquarters of the Roman governor and the main base of the Roman army. It was also a great international city on the route between East and West. Fronting on two seas, the gulf of Corinth on the north and the Saronic gulf on the south, it had two harbors, not joined as today by a canal, but linked by a pavement of rollers, along which the comparatively small ships of the time could be dragged from one harbor to the other. Thus Corinth in ancient times was the junction between East and West. It was the meeting place and the melting pot of men, cultures, sciences and trade, and likewise of sin and depravity. On the hill above the city rose the temple of Aphrodite with her many handmaids. Corinth was a city of great wealth and luxury, both materially and spiritually. Yet it was also a city of much material, spiritual, and moral poverty.

The two letters of St. Paul to the Corinthians preserved in the New Testament show the city in the same light. The Corinthians demanded culture and wisdom (1:12; 1 Cor. 1:17—2:16) and also eloquence (1:10; 11:6) in the preaching of the gospel. Various conflicting parties were formed in the church on the lines of the ancient philosophical schools, and St. Paul had a difficult task in restoring the unity of the church (10:1–18; 1 Cor. 1:10–31; 3:1–23). The Eucharist, in which the death of Christ was proclaimed, was in danger of losing its meaning at Corinth, with all the expensive carousing that accompanied it (1 Cor. 11:17–34). And then St. Paul had to deal with cases of gross immorality as nowhere else (12:21; 1 Cor. 5:1–12; 6:12–20).

In spite of everything, after great efforts he succeeded in establishing a large community at Corinth in a year and a half's missionary work, and the community flourished. The church founded in Corinth by the Apostle took firm root, and has existed without interruption to the present day.

In the summer of 53, St. Paul left Corinth and sailed to Ephesus, and then on to Palestine. In the spring of the next year, he started out from Antioch in Syria on his third missionary journey, which took him through Asia Minor and back to Ephesus, where he stayed for nearly three years, separated from Corinth only by the Aegean Sea (Acts 19:1—20:1).

The Aegean is not very wide, and there was constant traffic between Ephesus and Corinth, with messengers and news passing to and fro between St. Paul and the church of Corinth. When we examine the scattered indications, we find that St. Paul must have written at least four letters to Corinth in this period, which are usually designated as A, B, C, and D. Of these, A and C are lost, B and D preserved, appearing in our New Testament as the First and Second Epistles to the Corinthians. Some are inclined to think that parts of A and C may have been incorporated into the two letters to the Corinthians which survive.

The first epistle was written to put an end to unseemly partisan conflicts, to remedy some abuses in sexual matters, and to answer some questions which correspondents had asked about marriage and virginity, meat which had been offered in sacrifice to idols, the liturgy, and the resurrection. St. Paul's epistle was brought to Corinth by messengers.

Something must have happened then which almost caused a rupture between the Apostle and the community. This we deduce from certain hints in the second epistle, though it is not quite clear what they mean. St. Paul could take it for granted that his readers knew enough about the situation to understand him. But so much remains obscure for us that commentators are not always in agreement. It is generally admitted that St. Paul received in Ephesus disturbing news to the effect that false missionaries had penetrated the church of Corinth and were trying to undermine the community's allegiance towards its founding Apostle (10:1—12:13). This moved St. Paul to visit Corinth from Ephesus in the period between the first and second epistles, though there is no mention of this visit in the Acts of the Apostles (see 2:1; 12:14; 13:1). The visit, however, was hardly a success. The Corinthians made no decisive effort to rid themselves of St. Paul's opponents, and continued to listen to their criticisms and calumnies against the Apostle. In the course of the dispute, St. Paul seems to have been personally challenged and offended in one particular case, while the Corinthians made no move to call the offender to account and punish him (2:5-11).

St. Paul returned to Ephesus discouraged, full of grief and anxiety. Then he wrote a letter "with many tears" (2:3f.), demanding amendment and satisfaction. He sent Titus to Corinth with this letter, and Titus succeeded in bringing the community to reflect and repent (2:12f.; 7:5-7). This letter (= to the Corinthians, C) has not been preserved.

In the meantime, St. Paul had left Ephesus and met Titus, who was on his way back from Corinth, in Macedonia, probably at Philippi, where St. Paul was always particularly happy to stay (2:12f.). Here Titus gave him the good news which he had waited so anxiously to hear. Titus was able to say that the majority of the community at least were on the side of St. Paul. Full of joy and consolation (7:6), he responded to the Corinthians with another letter, the letter D, which is our Second Epistle to the Corinthians.

Each of the epistles of St. Paul which have come down to us has a special character and hence a special value of its own. At Corinth, St. Paul had to meet opponents who found fault with his personal qualities and his way of exercising office. They even went so far as to maintain that he was no true apostle, not having been called by Jesus during his earthly life, like the twelve. In discharging his office, he showed a lack of self-confidence and force (see on 10:1.10). St. Paul was therefore forced to defend his apostolic office, and did so in the Second Epistle to the Corinthians. Impelled by necessity, he created in so doing a theology of the apostolate in general. He described toil as the glory, poverty as the riches of this office. In a series of terse, moving confessions, he spoke of the contradictions which the office involved and which he had to bear (4:1–18; 6:3–10; 11:16—12:10). He gave the long list of trials which his office imposed on him. He was raised to the heights of heaven, but he had to endure, by the power of the Spirit, ceaseless and un-dreamed-of torments in a body racked by illness (4:11; 12:7).

In no other epistle was St. Paul forced to speak so much about himself as in the Second Epistle to the Corinthians. No other epistle is so personal and passionate. And so it reveals to us the resources which this extraordinary man had to draw upon. With all the anxiety of a father, he strived to make peace once more with the Corinthians. The love that constrained the Apostle was stronger than all misunderstandings and injuries. Then, with supreme irony, he presented his opponents as " apostles of the lie," and destroyed their pretensions with merciless blows. Such was the clearness and depth of his faith, such was his fellowship with the Lord in the Spirit, that he could judge, arrange, and organize everything, and yet endure everything. We can under-stand how this man could be the relentless opponent of so many enemies, and at the same time win the allegiance and love of so many men, indeed of whole communities.

St. Paul was fighting with all his might for a community in the Second Epistle to the Corinthians. What did this homeless wanderer own in the broad lands around the Mediterranean Sea? What could this destitute man call his own, except the communities of brothers which he had founded round its shores by preaching the gospel? All he possessed on earth was their confidence, their love, and their loyalty. He was burning himself out in their service, under indescribable dangers and hardships. Any weakening or loss of trust on the part of his communities must have caused him deep pain. This is proof of how truly great and human the Apostle was, since like all really great men, he was also great in his love.

But St. Paul's effort throughout was not to bind a community to his own person. " I am jealous for you," he assures his readers, " with God's jealousy. I betrothed you to one man, to lead you to Christ as a pure virgin. But I am afraid that just as the serpent deceived Eve in his cunning, so too your minds may be perverted from a single-minded devotion towards Christ " (11 : 2). St. Paul is striving to win a community, not for himself, but for Christ. They would be lost, not from him, but from Christ, and the community would not lose their Apostle St. Paul, but their Lord Jesus Christ.

No other epistle can make us sense the human and spiritual greatness of the Apostle like the Second Epistle to the Corinthians. This epistle places its author among the greatest men, the greatest theologians, and the greatest saints of the whole church.

No epistle of St. Paul is without its own particular difficulties of interpretation. In the Second Epistle to the Corinthians there are a number of difficulties and obscurities which arise from the

fact that St. Paul often confined himself to allusions to complicated situations which were known to his readers, but remain
unclear to us. Hence we cannot be quite sure exactly who were
the opponents with whom St. Paul is engaged in the epistle, or
what precisely was the matter disputed so fiercely (see chs.
10—13).

A second and much debated question, which we can do no
more than mention here, but which we cannot avoid mentioning, is that of the unity of the epistle.

According to 2:13, St. Paul is waiting for Titus in Macedonia.
The arrival of Titus is reported only in 7:5, which can be
harmonized with 2:13, though a certain gap remains. This has
to be explained, and some commentators suggest that 2:14—7:4
may be a later insertion. This can hardly be proven, however
(see 7:5). Other questions arise on account of the peculiarities of
6:14—7:1 (see 6:14). Chapters 8 and 9 deal with the collection
for Jerusalem, and they seem to do so, not in a continuous consideration, but by combining two separate but similar considerations. Were they originally two independent pieces of writing
(see 9:1)? The gravest and most difficult question is whether
and how the two parts of the letter, chs. 1—9 and chs. 10—13
were originally connected. With 7:16 St. Paul had made his
peace with the community of Corinth. In chs. 10—13, there was
another series of sharp attacks on his opponents (see on 10:1).

In view of these many questionable elements, many exegetes,
Catholic as well as Protestant, allow for the possibility that our
Second Epistle to the Corinthians was given its present unity
only by a later " editor."

St. Paul certainly did not himself publish his letters in the
form of a collection. This was only done later by others. The
epistles were obviously preserved at first in the church to which

he had addressed them. After the death of St. Paul, his letters were collected, so far as they were available, because their incomparable value was recognized. A Christian charged with this task also published the letters of St. Paul which were kept in the archives of the church of Corinth. But these letters were written on rather short rolls of papyrus, one letter taking up several rolls. It could happen that a roll was damaged at the beginning or the end. The editor had to fit the various rolls together, few of which probably contained any indication of which epistle they belonged to. In doing so, he may have—deliberately or mistakenly or accidentally or for whatever reason moved him—combined different letters of St. Paul, or fragments from various letters, to make up our present Second Epistle to the Corinthians.

A commentary in view of the spiritual reading of the New Testament need not take the matter into further account. One way or another, the epistle was written by St. Paul. And the church preserved it because it recognized that it would always remain an epistle to the whole church. It is in this sense that we have to interpret it.

OUTLINE

The Opening of the Letter (1:1-2)

THE OPENING OF THE LETTER (1:1-2)

  I. Sender and recipients (1:1)

  II. Greeting (1:2)

The Body of the Letter (1:3—13:10)

GOD'S CONSOLATION AND SALVATION (1:3-11)

  I. God's consolation (1:3-4)

  II. Union with Christ in suffering and in triumph (1:5-7)

  III. The rescue of the Apostle from mortal danger (1:8-11)

MISSION AND CHURCH ORDER (1:12—2:13)

  I. Paul's pure service (1:12-14)

    1. Paul's conduct (1:12)

    2. Paul's letters (1:13-14)

  II. The visit planned but not made (1:15—2:2)

    1. The intended journey (1:15-16)

    2. The sincerity of the Apostle (1:17-18)

    3. God's sincerity, revealed in Christ (1:19-20)

    4. God, the ground of truth in the church (1:21-22)

    5. The apostles, fellow workers of God (1:23-24)

    6. The community, the Apostle's joy (2:1-2)

  III. An earlier letter to Corinth (2:3-11)

    1. A letter written with tears (2:3-4)

    2. An offense and its punishment (2:5-6)

    3. But now pardon (2:7-11)

THE SECOND EPISTLE TO THE CORINTHIANS

THE OPENING OF THE LETTER
(1:1–2)

THE OPENING OF THE LETTER (1:1-2)

Letters have been written by all peoples and in all ages, and they have always taken on certain features and used set formulas. Thus in antiquity, at the time when the New Testament letters were being written, a standard form of letter had long been in use. It began by naming the sender and his rank or profession, then the recipients and their address. A greeting followed, containing good wishes for the recipient. For this reason, the opening lines of all St. Paul's letters are very similar. The heading is sometimes short and succinct, sometimes expanded more fully.

Sender and Recipients (1:1)

¹Paul, an apostle of Christ Jesus by the will of God, and our brother Timothy, to the church of God which is at Corinth, and to all the saints in the whole of Achaia.

In keeping no doubt with the whole intention of the letter, Paul stresses his mission and his mandate when he gives his name as the writer of the letter. He presents himself not of his own free choice, but as an apostle, that is, as a messenger of Christ, who was once the man Jesus and is now the exalted Lord. As envoy of another, it is not the Apostle's task to speak of himself, but of this other. He must deliver the message of his Lord, whether it is listened to or not: " We speak from God, in the sight of God, in Christ " (2:17). For his sake, Paul, as in this very letter, may be forced to use strong words and sharp arguments. His mission as an apostle imposes certain limits on him, just as it bestows on him strength and authority.

5

Along with himself Paul names in cordial unity his colleague Timothy, the fellow worker of Paul known to us from the Acts of the Apostles and from the epistles. But the letter was certainly not worked out in common by Paul and Timothy. It is entirely the work of Paul, as indeed follows from the way in which Paul speaks throughout the letter—in the first person singular. The naming of Timothy along with himself is an act of brotherly courtesy on the part of Paul.

The letter is addressed primarily to the church of God which is at Corinth. There is only one church of God, embracing all, but it is manifested and realized in the individual churches. And here the church does not mean the authorities or the priesthood, but the whole community. Looking beyond the city of Corinth, the letter is also addressed to all the saints in the whole of Achaia. Achaia is the name of the Roman province, which then included central Greece of the present day and the Peloponnesian peninsula. Paul had preached in this territory at Athens, but had succeeded in winning only a few to Christ (Acts 17:34). Other communities were no doubt established, as the faith and the church expanded rapidly, by its own vigor. Every Christian was also a missionary. The Christian community at Cenchreae near Corinth, mentioned in Rom. 16:1, must have been one of the churches which was founded in this way.

The Christians are all addressed as saints. What does the word mean? In the Bible of the Old and the New Testament, God is the Holy One, primordially and perpetually, and the real meaning of the word is, according to the Hebrew, that he is essentially apart from and different from the world which is his creation. He is "the wholly Other." Thus the prophet Isaiah saw God as the primordially holy when he saw him on his lofty throne with the seraphim around him, covering their faces and their whole

persons with their wings as they cried out to one another:
"Holy, holy, holy is the Lord of hosts. The whole earth is full
of his glory " (Is. 6:1-4). What the eternally holy God calls into
his realm, takes to himself, and fills with his presence is thereby
made holy: the holy angels, the holy city of Jerusalem, God's
chosen people in the ancient covenant, and God's chosen community in the new covenant, the church. When the church, and
hence Christians, are designated as holy, it does not mean
primarily a special moral steadfastness or a " saintly " perfection
attained by following the commandments of God. The title
signifies that Christians are called into God's community and
have become God's property. This of course implies and demands
the banishment of sin, since sin is incompatible with fellowship
with God the holy. The moral act of man follows from the gift
of God, which is there first. It is because God has sanctified man
that man can strive for a holy life.

Paul is obliged at times to reprimand his churches severely for
their weaknesses and sins. But at the same time, he calls the
members of these churches " the saints." Today the title of holy
is reserved for a few special persons. In the Roman church, the
pope is the Holy Father, the cardinals form a Sacred College,
and in another sense, the canonized saints are holy. In the New
Testament, all Christians are holy. Holiness is a dignity attributed
to them, but it is at the same time a duty which they must discharge by making the gift a reality in their lives.

Greeting (1 : 2)

[2]*Grace to you and peace, from God our Father and the Lord
Jesus Christ.*

The greeting wishes the church grace and peace. It was Paul no doubt who composed this formula of salutation, which then came into general use in the New Testament and has been constantly used in the church ever since. No other apostle pondered the nature of grace so much, or spoke so profoundly of it as God's turning to man to love him, forgive him, and create him anew. Paul therefore made the prayer for grace part of the greeting.

The wish " peace be with you " was the greeting used by the people of Israel since the time of the patriarchs, as it was in the East in general and as it has remained to the present day. The word " peace," however, does not merely indicate a mental attitude of repose and tranquility. It means reconciliation and peace with God, and hence the deliverance and salvation of men. For men it is the gift of God, for Christians it is a gift bestowed through Jesus Christ, the redeemer and Lord. Paul therefore names both the Father, who is the original source of peace, and Christ, who is the mediator and bringer of grace and peace.

The God who bestows such gifts is named " Father." This title is not confined to the New Testament and the Christian faith. The Old Testament used it, and indeed other religions at times address God as Father. But as a rule, God is addressed in Jewish prayers as King and Lord, while " Father " occurs very rarely. In no other religion is God called Father with such a sense of intimacy and assurance as in the New Testament. This was the teaching of Jesus. His disciples knew that the holy and almighty God was their loving Father, and that they could call him by this name. The " Our Father " is therefore truly the criterion of the disciple, a sort of basic charter for the church of Jesus Christ.

THE BODY OF THE LETTER
(1:3—13:10)

GOD'S CONSOLATION AND SALVATION
(1:3–11)

It was part of the formula of an ancient letter that the sender should add after the greeting a word of thanks to the godhead for the protection and blessing which it had accorded to the writer or the recipient. Paul often follows this custom in his letters. But the Apostle puts all his heart and conviction into the conventional formula. In his other letters, he thanks God for the graces given to the church to which he writes. But here the prayer dwells primarily on his own experience. This is characteristic of a letter which is almost entirely concerned with a deep personal experience of the Apostle, and which is marked more than any other by the personality of the author. Contrary to his usual custom of starting with the events and conditions of the church, here Paul allows his own stirring experiences to intrude into the foreground in the prayer.

God's Consolation (1:3–4)

³Blessed be the God and Father of our Lord Jesus Christ, the Father of mercies and God of all consolation . . .

God is praised as the God and Father of Jesus Christ. He is the God who sent Jesus Christ and revealed himself in him, the God whom Jesus preached and to whom Jesus also prayed. He is the Father, whose Son Jesus knew and proclaimed himself to be, the Father, whom Jesus taught men to recognize as their own. He is also the Father of mercies and God of all consolation.

That is God's nature: to give comfort, not to judge and condemn, but to have mercy. Indeed, he is the creator and source
of all mercy, from whom flows all consolation. All mercy and
consolation among men is ultimately derived from God, since
it is because they themselves have had mercy from God that
they can have mercy on others.

*4. . . . who consoles us in all our tribulation, so that we can
comfort others in any tribulation they suffer, by the comfort by
which we ourselves have been consoled by God.*

From God as the source of consolation, consolation streams into
the church. God consoles the Apostle, so that he can in turn
bring comfort to others and to the whole church. He is no doubt
the servant of all, but we can already note another essential
element of the apostolic office: the Apostle is mediator between
God and the church. God gives his consolation through the
Apostle.

Consolation is the help in the many pressing tribulations.
The Bible often speaks of the many trials and tribulations of
the people of God, and of the just and pious. According to the
New Testament, this is part of Christian existence in this age
and world. God's servants who have reached their goal have
always arrived there from great tribulation (Rev. 7:14). In the
last resort, it is always the one tribulation of the end of days,
which has already begun, and out of which the final salvation
of God is born. Even the Apostle, indeed, the Apostle above all,
must share in this tribulation. He sees all his woes as forerunners
of that ultimate distress which is death. But distress is overcome
by the consolation given by God (1:4), by the superabundant
joy of the Holy Spirit (8:2), and by the hope of the glory to
come (4:17f.).

Union with Christ
in Suffering and in Triumph (1:5–7)

⁵For as the sufferings of Christ are imparted to us in abundance, so too through Christ our consolation is abundant.

In the communion of faith, no one is alone in distress, no one receives consolation for himself alone. All that is done forms part of the fellowship of Christ (1:5), as it does of the church (1:6).

The truth here affirmed by the Apostle is constantly repeated throughout the New Testament: the sufferings of Christians are associated with the sufferings of Christ. They are part of them. They even complete them. This unity of the sufferings of Christ and Christians is explained by three reasons, which bring us from the surface to the heart of things.

The persecutions, pains, and tribulations which the disciple has to undergo are visibly and outwardly similar to, indeed the same as, those which Christ had to bear. Christ himself had told his disciples that they would have to drink the cup of sufferings which he had to drink, and be baptized in the baptism of suffering with which he had to be baptized (Mk. 10:38f.). The saying about bearing witness unto the shedding of blood means precisely that the disciple must share the fate of his Lord and master: "If they have persecuted me, they will also persecute you" (Jn. 15:20). Paul thinks of his scarred body and his life marked with suffering when he says: "I bear the marks of Jesus on my body" (Gal. 6:17), and more emphatically still: "I always carry in my body the mortal sufferings of Jesus" (4:10).

Suffering comes upon the disciple for the sake of Christ. The sufferings are undergone because of Christ, and their full meas-

ure is borne in loyalty to Christ. For the sake of Christ the
Apostle is a fool in the eyes of the world (1 Cor. 4:10). For the
sake of Jesus he is delivered over to death (4:11). The martyrs
give their lives as witnesses to the word of God and to Jesus
Christ (Rev. 6:9; 20:4).

But it goes deeper. The disciple suffers in unity with Christ
and as a member of Christ. Christ suffers in the Christian, and
the Christian suffers in Christ. When Christ appeared to the
persecutor of the church on the road to Damascus, he told him
that he was persecuting the Lord Christ himself in the church
(Acts 9:4f.). In the Epistle to the Romans, the Apostle sees
immersion in the waters of baptism and emerging from them
as an image of Jesus' being buried in death and rising again
(Rom. 6:3–11). In baptism, death and resurrection are mysteri-
ously portrayed and accomplished in the believer. The sufferings
of Christ and of the Christian form such a unity that Paul can
say: According to God's plan of salvation, there is a preordained
measure of suffering to be filled. Christ has done one part; the
other is to be completed by the disciples. " Now I rejoice in my
sufferings for you, and fill up what is still wanting to the sufferings of Christ, for you, in my flesh, for the body of Christ,
which is the church " (Col. 1:24).

In this fellowship of suffering, Christ brings about the consolation of suffering. The fellowship finally brings about fellowship in glory. " He was crucified in weakness, but lives by the
power of God. And we too are weak in him, but we live with
him by the power of God, which he gives us " (13:4). Fellowship in experiencing the sufferings of Christ also guarantees the
power of experiencing his resurrection. To have been shaped in
the likeness of his death means also to experience with him the
resurrection from the dead. Indeed, this resurrection already

takes place here and now in the new life of faith, to be completed in the resurrection at the end of time. Thus in common
suffering, unity of life with Christ is realized: " I live no more,
but Christ lives in me. The life I now live in the flesh, I live in
faith in the Son of God, who loved me and delivered himself up
for me " (Gal. 2:20).

*If we are afflicted, it is for your comfort and salvation. If we
are consoled, it is for your comfort, which is at work when you
endure the same sufferings as we suffer.*

All that Paul suffers and undergoes is for the church. Fellowship with the one Christ implies and brings about the fellowship
of Christians with one another. Thus the Apostle's endurance of
suffering becomes a blessing for the church. And when he receives consolation, this too is given him so that he can transmit
it to others by his preaching, his letters, and the example of his
life. Others too receive consolation and the salvation which is
the end and object of the consolation.

Sufferings abide for the Apostle as for the church. They are
the same for both, and they are universal and inevitable. But
God embodies his consolation in them, and the power of patient
endurance. When Paul speaks of sufferings, he thinks no doubt
of the menaces and the assaults launched by the enemies of the
faith, of which the Christians in Corinth are the victims just as
much as Paul is everywhere (2 Thess. 2:14). He may also be
thinking of the human and spiritual inadequacies which he
as a sick man feels in a special way (12:7.9), but which every
man comes up against every day (Rom. 8:38). Behind everything, however, are the onslaughts of the " malignant enemy,"
who seeks to thwart the Apostle (2: 11; 1 Thess. 2:18) just as he

tries to pervert the faithful (1 Cor. 10:13; Eph. 6:11f.). " But
in all things we conquer overwhelmingly " (Rom. 8:37).

*⁷So our hope for you is steadfast, since we know that just as you
share our sufferings you also share our consolation.*

From his consolation the Christian gains the strength of patience,
and from patience he goes on to the confidence of unshakable
hope. Paul experiences this himself, and he knows that the
Corinthians are assured of it. He knows how the Christians
feel with him in his tribulation—Titus no doubt told him of
their sympathy (7:6). But at the same time he could have told
him that the church is not cast down. Knowledge of how things
are provides certainty of how things will always be: that suffering and affliction will always be consoled and redeemed, as was
also promised by the Lord in the beatitudes of the Sermon on
the Mount (Mt. 5:3–12).

The Rescue of the Apostle
from Mortal Danger (1:8–11)

*⁸For we do not wish to leave you in ignorance, my brothers, about
the tribulation which came upon us in Asia—that we were so
grievously burdened, beyond what our strength could bear, that
we even despaired of life.*

After these general thoughts on how distress and comfort act
upon each other, Paul alludes to some special calamity. He
knows how well the experience of the Corinthians bears out the
general truth. Now he tells them that it has also been proved

true in his own life. He had had recent evidence of it in a very special way when he was rescued from danger of death. Paul only makes allusions to this event, and we do not know exactly what he means. All we know is that he was in grave danger. And even here we do not know whether the plural he uses is only the writer's way of speaking of himself, or, as is more probable, whether he is speaking of one or more of his companions also. The description does not seem to suggest one of the deadly dangers of a journey which are quickly over, such as occur during a river crossing or when a ship founders—dangers which Paul indeed experienced often enough (11 : 25f.). We should rather think of a grave danger which hung over them for a longer period. Paul and his companions had perhaps fallen into the hands of a hostile crowd and been roughly handled or had been thrown into prison, charged with a capital offense. In any case, the situation of the missionaries was something " beyond their strength " to bear. They saw no way out of it and gave themselves up for lost.

Paul addresses his Christians as " brothers," which is the way Christians think and speak of each other in the whole of the New Testament. This follows the custom of the Jewish people, who felt themselves to be one great family united by ties of blood to the patriarchs. Jesus uses the word to describe the community of his disciples. They must think of themselves as a band of brothers (Mt. 23 : 8). Jesus himself spoke of his disciples as his brothers and sisters (Mk. 3 : 35). Above all was the heavenly Father, the one Father of all : " He who does the will of my Father in heaven, he is brother and sister and mother to me " (Mt. 12 : 50). United in a new fellowship of faith, the brotherhood of Christians was no longer merely the natural bond of blood, but a new creation.

As a name and form of address, " brother " and " sister " fell
into disuse in the ordinary lives of Christians, to survive however
in the religious life. Outside religious houses, it has remained
normal to address members of religious orders or congregations
as " brothers " and " sisters." From nursing orders of nuns, the
title " sister " passed on to certain nurses in hospitals. The fact
that we may still address religious as " brother " and " sister "
is, therefore, a relic of biblical speech in which the spirit of the
New Testament is still at work. When sisters in convents and
hospitals still have this title today, it is a reminder of the his-
torical fact: that humaneness throughout the world is a child of
Christian charity.

*[9]Indeed, we had already uttered the sentence of death for our-
selves, so that we no longer relied on ourselves, but on God who
raises the dead. [10]He rescued us from such mortal perils, and
he will deliver us. We hope in him, that he will continue to
rescue us.*

The faith of Israel, like that of the church, knows and proclaims
God as he who raises up the dead. Elsewhere Paul says of God
that it is he " who gives life to the dead " (Rom. 4:17). The
Apostle is using, it would seem, a formula from an ancient
Jewish prayer. In the *Shemone Esre* (" the eighteen petitions "),
which is still used in the synagogue, praise of God is uttered in
the form: " You live for eternity, you raise up the dead. You care
for the living, you give life to the dying." If so, Paul would not
be thinking, say, of the resurrection of Jesus from the dead, as
one might easily suppose, but of the general resurrection, when
God raises the dead at the end of time. This God, the conqueror
of death, has delivered Paul from danger of death. Paul has

learned that God's hand was at work, to dispose and guide, where according to human estimation there was only the direst peril. Paul could recognize, and take to heart for ever, that God is always the Lord, who leads out to freedom when all ways seem blocked, who brings out of death into life. Hence in the Bible God is simply called " the deliverer " (Ps. 18 : 3; 70 : 6).

It is true that we men are doomed to death and destruction with our whole world. But in our hopeless state, the word of God bids us hope for God's great miracle, which conquers and will conquer death by life.

[11]*And there you will also work together for us by your prayer, so that from many lips thanksgiving will be offered for us by many for the grace bestowed upon us.*

Paul will be in danger again, and again only God's power will be able to rescue him. So he asks for the help of his Christians' prayer. The Apostle knows with perfect certainty that prayers offered for someone can surround him with protection and help. He speaks first of the prayer of petition, but goes on at once and still more emphatically to speak of thanksgiving. For he who believes, every prayer is really a thanksgiving, because he is constantly experiencing the grace of God. He turns everything into a " eucharist." Thus the church is to be a great fellowship of prayer, or rather, a great choir of thanksgiving, having in mind the apostolic office and the mission, and putting its cares before God.

MISSION AND CHURCH ORDER (1:12—2:13)

In this part of the letter, which leads on to a further discussion, Paul brings up some questions and difficulties which trouble the relationship between himself and the church of Corinth. They are probably personal matters to begin with, but they affect in principle the whole mission and the good order of the church. The passage also gives us a glimpse of the origin and development of an apostolic church, and of the beginnings of church history in general.

Paul's Pure Service (1:12–14)

After his cordial words of friendship, which showed the Apostle and his community united in a fellowship of prayer and consolation, Paul enters on the field of controversy, which the Corinthians have forced upon him, and to which he returns constantly throughout the letter, till he finally brings it to an end in 10:1—13:10 with the utmost energy. He first defends himself against the charge of making worldly wisdom his rule of conduct (1:12), and of writing dishonest letters (1:13). He stresses on the contrary the single-mindedness of his intentions.

Paul's Conduct (1: 12)

¹²*This is our boast: the testimony of our conscience, that we have acted in the holiness and sincerity of God, not in worldly wisdom, but in the grace of God, in our dealings with the world, but especially with you.*

Paul asked the church to pray and give thanks with him and for him. He merits such thanksgiving and intercession, for his work is blameless. He can even boast of it. That is Paul's statement, even though he knows and repeats constantly in his letters how questionable it is to assert that anyone is ever allowed to boast. But boasting can be false or true. The pride that tries to rely on itself and boast of human achievement before God is empty and false. Of such boasting Paul says firmly and clearly: " It is excluded " (Rom. 3 : 27). " Before God, no one can boast " (1 Cor. 1 : 29). If boasting is allowed at all, it can only be " to glory in the Lord " (1 Cor. 1 : 31) and " in the cross of the Lord " (Gal. 6 : 14). Man can only boast because God has saved him from the wreck of his life and work, as he led Christ to life through his death on the cross. It is the pride in which man looks away from himself, to fix his eyes on the future as it comes from God. In this tension between true and false boasting, there is a place for the boast to which Paul is forced to return again and again in the Second Epistle to the Corinthians, in face of the hostility shown him. As he says at the end, he does not boast of his own strength, but of his weakness, in which God's power is displayed.

Examining his conscience, Paul can boast of holiness and sincerity: not his own, indeed, but the holiness and sincerity of God. He had not acquired these virtues by his own ability. The grace of God had produced them in him. The holiness of the Apostle is simply the love with which God calls men and binds them to himself. It is a dignity which belongs to all Christians (see 1 : 1). Like holiness, sincerity too is first of all an attribute of God, since he alone is completely pure and without stain.

Because of the grace of God, Paul can also say with assurance that his conduct had not been dictated by worldly wisdom—

" fleshly " in the Greek. His dealings " with the world," that is, wherever he worked, were free, he knew, from such motives. But in Corinth above all this should have been clear. Paul had been there a year and a half, long enough for the Corinthians to get to know him well. The difficult situation in Corinth, attested by the two epistles to the Corinthians, had enabled him to demonstrate his sincerity better than anywhere else. Paul may also be thinking of something of which he reminds the Corinthians again and again (11:7; 1 Cor. 9:6): during all his time in Corinth he earned his living by his own hands. He had never claimed his right, as a missionary, to be supported by the community. It should therefore be clear that as a missionary he had no interest in personal gain. His only object was to serve the community.

Paul's Letters (1:13-14)

[13]*We write nothing to you, except what you read and what you know [from our letters]. But I hope that you will come to know fully,* [14]*as indeed you already know in part: that we are your boast, as you are ours, on the day of our Lord Jesus.*

It was his letters that had exposed Paul to the charge of worldly wisdom. He had already been obliged to defend himself in an earlier letter against misunderstandings and deliberate distortions of his meaning. We can tell from his way of defending himself what the accusation was: his letters were not straightforward; he writes and says one thing, but he has something else in mind.

Paul also knows, however, that the Corinthians have understood him correctly, at least to some extent. He is sure that in the end they will understand him fully. This is not merely because they will be using their intelligence better, humanly speaking. The Apostle is thinking of the last day, when the Lord comes again, in the near future. Everything will be cleared up in the light of the day of judgment. And the whole world will be able to see that the church of Corinth, which the Apostle founded with so much labor and cared for with so much love, is the Apostle's title to glory. And Paul will also be the boast of the church of Corinth, which will be proud of its Apostle and founder.

The Visit Planned but Not Made (1:15–2:2)

Another grievance of the Corinthians was that Paul was supposed to have promised visits which he never paid, abandoning his plans after having announced that he was traveling. He admits that he changed his original plan of paying a second visit to Corinth. But this is no reason for accusing him of being unreliable. He knows that in Christ God has uttered his clear and unambiguous " Yes " to the world, and that the apostle who is God's envoy must also be sincere and reliable (1 : 18f.). His only reason for dropping the proposed visit was to spare the Corinthians (1 : 23).

The Intended Journey (1:15–16)

[15]*Confident of this, I intended to come to you earlier, so that you would receive grace for the second time,* [16]*and then to go on from you to Macedonia, and visit you once more on my way back from Macedonia, so that you could accompany me to Judea.*

When Paul had planned his journey, he had been quite sure that he and his work were understood and welcomed with confidence by the Corinthians. With this in mind, he had planned a second visit to Corinth, intending to go on to Macedonia, then to return to Corinth and finally to go to Judea, with an escort of Corinthians. Paul had given a somewhat different version of his plans in the First Epistle to the Corinthians, the main point being that he had promised to spend a longer time with the Corinthians (1 Cor. 16:5-9). He had in fact changed his plans, and the community was not happy about the change.

This second visit to Corinth should have been another occasion of grace for the Corinthians. Paul is not speaking of grace in the sense in which a visit from a great personage is sometimes described as an act of " grace and favour." He means that the visit of an apostle is a means by which God bestows grace on the church. The apostle is not only a teacher and preacher, he is also mediator of grace between God and man. His presence in the community opens up the floodgates of God's mercy. Paul shows again and again how conscious he is of being a priest in the service of God and the community, as when he says: " I know that when I come to you, I shall come in the fullness of the blessing of Christ " (Rom. 15:29).

The Sincerity of the Apostle (1:17-18)

¹⁷*When I wanted to do this, was I in any way casual? Or when I make plans, do I do so in a fleshly way, so that I say Yes and No [at the same time]?* ¹⁸*As true as God, our word to you is not Yes and No [at the same time].*

Paul changed his plans and cancelled his trip. He was then

accused in Corinth of forming his plans in a casual and fleshly way, that is, inconsiderately and selfishly. His Yes changes to No according to his mood.

We find it easy enough to imagine that Paul might have had good reasons to change his plans, or that he might have had no option but to do so. Does it not seem that he is being reproached for very little? If the Corinthians take offense, they must be very malicious or very possessive, at least those of them who find fault with Paul. But Paul is deeply hurt by the charge, and takes up very seriously the whole duty of truthfulness and sincerity. Indeed, it is magnificent to see how he can take, as he does here, come trifling question of everyday life, and treat it in the light of the great principles of the Christian faith. If we follow carefully the answer he gives, we shall not be far from grasping how grave is the obligation of the preacher of the gospel to be sincere, and indeed, how much all Christians are obliged to sincerity.

Paul does not deny that he changed his plans and did not carry out his promises, but he rejects emphatically the charge of having acted lightly. He calls on God as his witness. God is true. And since the Apostle is the servant of God, he knows that God's own truthfulness is at stake, as it were, and that he must embody it.

God's Sincerity, Revealed in Christ (1 : 19-20)

¹⁹*For the Son of God, Christ Jesus, who was preached among you by us, by Silvanus and Timothy and myself—he was not Yes and No. The Yes came to be, in him.*

The apostles were also bound to speak the truth in all sincerity, because of the coming of the Son of God, in whom God uttered his Yes to history and the world (1 : 20). The apostles echo this Yes in their preaching. Their own word and their whole life must be in keeping with the gospel which they proclaim. And the image of the Lord Jesus Christ remains an example which obliges all Christians as well as the apostles. The life of the disciple must be the imitation of Christ. This is true ever since Jesus called his disciples with the words: " Come, follow me."

20All the promises of God that there are—in him is the Yes. Hence too, through him, the Amen to God, to his glory, on our lips.

Christ is the great Yes of God, because in him all God's promises are marvelously ratified and fulfilled. Paul is certainly thinking in the first place of the promises of salvation, which God made to the people of Israel, his chosen people, from the beginning. They were the promises of the blessings which God would shower on his people, and indeed, on all peoples, when he establishes his glorious kingdom. He was to raise up in Israel the great teacher and saviour, the Messiah. Israel was to attain what it had striven for for many centuries by the observation of the law: redemption from sin and righteousness in the sight of God.

The great promises of salvation have now been fulfilled in Christ. But Paul is also convinced that many particular events in the history of salvation have found their fulfillment. He believes, for instance, that the two great sacraments of the church, baptism and the Eucharist, were typified long ago by Israel's passage through the Red Sea and by the manna which was

their food in the desert (1 Cor. 10:1-4). Paul sees a prophecy
of the world-wide preaching of the gospel in the words of the
psalm: " Their voice rings out to the whole world, and their
words carry to the ends of the earth " (Ps. 19:5; cf. Rom.
10:18). Thus the whole New Testament interprets the Old
in terms of Christ and the church. All the promises of God
are now fulfilled.

But Paul is also convinced that God did not leave the pagans
wholly without light in the past. He also gave testimony of himself to them, both in creation, which gives some hint of the
Creator (Rom. 1:18-32), and man's conscience, by which God's
law is written in the hearts of men (Rom. 2:14f.). The pagans'
hopes of salvation have also been fulfilled.

God's great Yes to the world is taken up by the church. As is
still the custom today, the church to which Paul wrote responded
to the prayers and hymns of the congregation with the affirma-
tive cry of " Amen," which means, Yes, so it is. In its Amen,
the church expresses its faith, in an answer which testifies that
God's words are true and are constantly being fulfilled. It is the
Yes to the Yes of God. In Paul too, as a member of the church,
this great Yes cannot but be valid and efficacious.

The Yes of the church rings out through Christ. Prayer is
brought about by Christ. Genuine prayer is never just the work
of man. In prayer, the Spirit of Christ who is bestowed on the
faithful and dwells in them, speaks to God. It is only in this
Spirit that we are enabled to say: Father, dear Father (Rom.
8:15). And Christ himself, the heavenly high priest of his
church, is the mediator who brings the prayers of the community
to the Father (Heb. 2:17). Hence the church still prays today
as it did from the start: " through our Lord Jesus Christ, thy
Son, who liveth and reigneth with thee, eternal God, in the

unity of the Holy Spirit, for ever and ever. Amen " (cf. Rom.
1 : 8; 1 Pet. 4 : 11; Jude 25).

God, the Ground of Truth in the Church (1 : 21–22)

*21But it is God who has founded us on Christ along with you,
who has also anointed us . . .*

Truth in the church is ultimately founded on the one true God,
in whom all, both the Apostle and the Corinthians, live and have
their being. But God gives his church stability, perpetuity, and
oneness. When Paul describes how God founds and builds up
the church, he is obviously thinking of baptism. The Spirit is
bestowed in baptism, which was therefore spoken of metaphorically as the anointing with the Spirit. This gave rise very early
to the ceremony of anointing at baptism with blessed oil, a rite
still in use at the present day.

*22. . . and put his seal on us, and placed the Spirit in our hearts
as a pledge of the future.*

Baptism is also spoken of metaphorically as the act of stamping
with a seal. To put a seal on something is to acknowledge it,
to mark it as one's own, to take it under one's protection.
By baptism, man is removed from the realm of the powers of
evil, made God's property and placed under God's protection.
Both the Old and the New Testament describe in impressive
imagery how God's elect and holy ones are redeemed and made
perfect by being stamped with the seal of salvation (Ezek. 9 : 4–6;
Rev. 7 : 2–8; 14 : 1).

Baptism is the means whereby the Spirit of God is given. With regard to the present time, the seal and the gift of the Spirit are the guarantee of truth and sincerity in the fellowship of the church. But as regards the future, this Spirit is a pledge, the first instalment, so to speak, of the great, final gift which God will bestow when he fulfills all things. This token is the proof that God is determined to bestow the full riches of his gift at the end. The Spirit is a pledge, because he has been placed in the hearts of the faithful, so that they already experience the world to come and are already assured of the world to come.

The text brings together Christ, God the Father, and the Spirit in close unity—the names which we pronounce together today when we profess our faith in the Holy Trinity. They are not yet exactly the words we use: Father, Son, and Holy Spirit, and our text does not keep necessarily to the order to which we are accustomed. But God works on the world and in the world as the eternal God, who is revealed in the Son, and present in the world in the power of the Spirit.

The Apostles, Fellow Workers of God (1:23-24)

²³*But I call God to witness, against my life, that it was to spare you that I did not come to Corinth.*

After his solemn assurances and affirmations of principle, Paul gives the exact reason for not coming to Corinth. First he appeals once more (1 : 18) to God, to bear witness against his life. To say this is to stake one's life on the truth of what one says.

The reason, therefore, why Paul gave up his original plan and cancelled his visit to Corinth is that he wished to spare the

Corinthians. He would have had to open his visit with severe reprimands.

²⁴Not that we lord it over your faith; we are rather helpers of your joy. For you are firm in your faith.

In speaking as he did, Paul was fully aware of his right to give commands and even to deal out punishment. But he is afraid of his words being misunderstood and distorted. He has no doubt already heard of such comments (10:8; 13:10; 1 Cor. 7:35). Conscious though he is of his right, he can never make the possession of such power a subject of self-congratulation. Stating a fundamental principle about his office, he affirms that he is not lord, but servant of the community. He says elsewhere in the same way: " Although I am free, I made myself the servant in all things, to win many " (1 Cor. 9:19). Our Lord had already spoken to the same effect when he said to his disciples: " He who would be great among you, let him be your servant; and he who would be first among you, let him be servant of all " (Mk. 10:43).

Thus Paul ministers to the joy of the community. Joy is characteristic of the Christian: " Rejoice in the Lord always. Again I say to you: rejoice " (Phil. 4:4). Joy can even be a way of describing Christianity, which is " righteousness and peace and joy in the Holy Spirit " (Rom. 14:17). Paul helps with this joy, which is really brought about by another, God. When Paul says of the apostle that he cooperates with God's work, he is making a truly lofty claim. But he makes it again and again: " We are God's fellow workers. You are God's field, God's building " (1 Cor. 3:9). He calls Timothy " God's fellow worker in the gospel " (1 Thess. 3:2). God himself founded the community of Corinth by the gift of faith. And because the church believes, it is firm and strong. In faith it is face to face with God, and no man may intrude into this intimacy. Faith can tolerate no man as Lord.

The Community, the Apostle's Joy (2 : 1–2)

²:¹So I had determined not to come to you again in sorrow. ²If I sadden you, who shall give me joy, except those who are saddened by me?

Being and wishing to be servant of joy, Paul decided not to visit Corinth. He would have had to cause pain to the church, as he had had to do once already. Paul is apparently alluding to a journey to Corinth which we know nothing about, except what we can gather from his hints. But it must have involved sharp clashes between himself and some members of the community, which the Apostle found very painful.

But it would have grieved Paul very much if he had found himself forced to cause pain to the Corinthians. This was another reason why he did not come—to spare himself pain. He too desires joy, not sorrow. If he cannot find joy in his communities, where else is he to look for it? With the same cordial warmth with which he addresses the Corinthians here, he also assures the churches at Thessalonica (1 Thess. 2 : 19f.) and Philippi (Phil. 4 : 1) that they are and must be his joy.

An Earlier Letter to Corinth (2 :3–11)

Paul continues to defend himself against the reproaches of the Corinthians. He recalls what happened. The circumstances were so

unhappy that he decided not to come. He wrote a letter instead, to
clear up an incident which affected the Apostle profoundly. However,
the community has by now condemned and punished the guilty
party, who is sorry for his offense. Paul for his part now urges forgiveness and clemency with regard to the offender. He does not
describe the incident in detail. The Corinthians know what and
whom he is talking about. And the Apostle wishes to let by-gones be
by-gones. His references to the incident are so vague that we now
find it hard to decipher his hints fully and correctly.

A Letter Written with Tears (2 : 3–4)

*3Hence I wrote a letter, so that when I came, I should not be
saddened by those who should have given me joy. For I have
this confidence in all of you, that my joy is the joy of you all.
4In great distress and anxiety of heart, I wrote to you with many
tears, not to make you sad, but so that you would know the love
which I bear you so abundantly.*

Paul thought that by writing a letter, which was painful enough,
he could avoid a still further visit to Corinth. Only joy and
peace should reign between Paul and his community. To be
deprived of them grieves the Apostle deeply. He is a tireless
worker and a dour fighter, but he is also an affectionate and
sensitive human being.

Paul has no intention of trying to lord it over his communities.
He wrote that sharp letter of reprimand with many tears, and
in great distress. If he had to pain the Corinthians, he felt deeply
pained himself. The letter was in fact an open proof of the
Apostle's continuing love for the Corinthians. It was his love for
the community that made his anxiety for it so overwhelming.

An Offense and Its Punishment (2 : 5–6)

⁵*But if anyone caused me pain, he did not pain me, but to some extent—I do not wish to exaggerate—all of you.*

Paul continues to allude to an incident in Corinth which had clouded the relationship between the Apostle and the community. Someone, a member of the community, had committed a grave offense, of such a nature as to affect and injure Paul himself. The offender may have made Paul his immediate target, or he may have wronged one of his fellow workers, such as Timothy, and thereby Paul indirectly. But the Apostle reminds his readers that he was not the only person affected. Paul's honor and standing are the honor and standing of the whole community. And all are of course grieved and stricken when a member of the community stumbles and falls. The community, however, did not intervene as it ought to have done, at least in Paul's estimation. If Paul had been there, he would have had to insist on strict church discipline. His hope had been to avoid such harsh measures, by writing a letter of warning and reproof, the letter, in fact, which he had written with many tears.

⁶*For the person in question, this punishment inflicted by the majority is enough . . .*

Since then, however, the majority of the community had imposed a punishment on the guilty party. The punishment is not to be so severe as to be harsh, and the enforcement of church discipline may not expose the offender to danger.

Thus we have a glimpse of how communities were governed in the apostolic church. The majority called for a punishment. Presumably the community had assembled to discuss the case, and voted on a certain proposal. A minority rejected it, but accepted the result of the vote, as law and order demanded and still demands in a community. We are not told whether the minority asked for a milder or a more severe punishment; either is possible. It follows that Paul did not simply lay down the law in his communities. He left them free to take their own decisions.

But Now Pardon (2 : 7–11)

[7]. . . so that [now] on the contrary you must forgive and console him, so that the person in question may not be plunged into excessive grief. [8]So I urge you, let love be your rule of conduct when dealing with him.

Condemnation and punishment have attained their end, which was to bring about repentance and conversion in the offender. With the anxious love of the true shepherd of souls, Paul now insists on other measures. He urges reconciliation, kindness, and love. The sinner is not to be the victim of an excessive grief. Paul knows that a man can be overwhelmed by too much distress. The object of church discipline is not final exclusion from the community, but forgiveness of the fault and the re-establishment of fellowship. The sinner is to be taken back into the community.

[9]That indeed is why I wrote to you [telling you to punish him]: to test your quality, to see whether you are obedient in all things. [10a]But anyone who is forgiven by you is also forgiven by me.

The letter which Paul wrote with tears was also intended to serve, in the last resort, the fellowship of love. The letter had demanded the punishment of the guilty party. But its ultimate object was not the punishment, but the testing of the Corinthians. Their whole attitude of obedience to the Apostle was to be given a chance to prove itself. And it stood the test. All that now remains is to show forgiveness and love. This Paul must do as well as the community.

10b*For I too, if I had anything to forgive, have granted forgiveness for your sake in the sight of Christ . . .*

In handling the difficult case of an offense committed by a member of the community, only Paul and the Corinthians have been named so far as actors, and the motives given were only general considerations of humanity. But now the curtain is suddenly drawn back, to show the background of everything that happens in the church. Everything takes place in the sight of Christ. He is enthroned as Lord and Judge. The Apostle and the church are standing before him, and all they do must be able to bear his gaze.

This sovereign does indeed demand law and order: " Whatever you bind or loose on earth, shall also be bound or loosed in heaven " (Mt. 18:18). But his first commandment is that of service and love in the community of the disciples. The life and teaching of Christ establish the law of forgiveness and reconciliation in the church: " Forgive one another, if anyone has a complaint against another. As the Lord has forgiven you, so you must also forgive " (Col. 3:13). And this Lord is mediator of the forgiveness of God: " If anyone sins, we have an intercessor before the Father, Jesus Christ, the just " (1 Jn. 2:1). Christ, in whose sight the church lives, commands forgiveness among men. And makes it valid before God.

[11]. . . so that we may not be overreached by Satan. For we are
well acquainted with his designs.

There is still another actor on the stage where history and the
history of salvation take place, Satan, the antagonist of the
church as of its Lord. The New Testament often speaks of his
disturbing and destructive aims and activity. He is a danger not
only to a guilty sinner, but also to Paul himself and the whole
church. If charity fails in the church, Satan can worm his way
in. He is the enemy of peace and love. Hatred and confusion
are what he aims at. Through all the time of the church, he is
the enemy on the watch. " Be sober and vigilant. Your adversary,
the devil, goes around like a roaring lion, seeking someone to
devour. Resist him, firm in faith " (1 Pet. 5:8). The adversary
will be swept away only at the end of time, at the coming of the
Lord. " Then the Lord Jesus will sweep away the lawless one
by the breath of his mouth, and destroy him by the manifestation of his coming " (2 Thess. 2:8).

Journeys of Paul in Troas and Macedonia (2:12–13)

During the uncertainties of the incident just described, Paul was
plagued by his anxiety for the church in Corinth at every step of his
missionary journeys. He could be at ease nowhere, till Titus finally
reached him in Macedonia with good news from Corinth.

[12]But when I came to Troas to preach the gospel of Christ, and
a door opened to me in the Lord . . .

To spare himself and the Corinthians and to avoid strife, Paul
decided not to travel to Corinth himself (1:23). Instead, probably

from Ephesus (Acts 19:1), he wrote the famous "Letter with tears" to Corinth (2:3f.). Titus, the trusty fellow worker of Paul who is often mentioned in Paul's letters, was to take the letter to Corinth and then report to Paul on the result. Paul had arranged to meet him at Troas, the ancient city on the west coast of Asia Minor, to hear his news. But even while he was waiting, Paul felt obliged to go on with his missionary work. He describes its success vividly: "A door opened to me" (cf. 1 Cor. 16:9: "In Ephesus a great and promising door opened to me"). A door opened in the strange town to the missionary's knocking. He finds hearers, he finds shelter, a place to preach in and offer divine worship.

But these visible happenings are only the externals of the inward event: ears and hearts open to the word of God. It is not the Apostle who opens the door. It opens to him. The missionary knows that it is not his own capability that brings success. Christ the Lord is at work wherever the gospel is listened to. Everything takes place in the Lord.

[13]. . . *I had no peace of mind, because I did not find my brother Titus there. So I bade them farewell and set out for Macedonia.*

But there was no rest for Paul. He could not prolong his stay in Troas and go on with his mission there. He was waiting too impatiently for Titus and the news which he was to bring back from Corinth. In the conflict between the new tasks in Troas and his anxiety for the older community in Corinth, he came down on the side of Corinth. He left Troas, crossed the Bosphorus and made for Macedonia, thus going a good part of the way to meet Titus on his journey from Corinth. Paul waited for his helper in one of the communities of Macedonia, probably

Philippi. Paul's anxiety for the church of Corinth was therefore very great, even though he was slow about paying it a visit.

This text gives an idea of the conflicting claims of pastoral work in a definite community and the onward thrust of the mission, which Paul had to weigh here. The conflict must often have arisen in the life of this enterprising and fiery Apostle.

One might have expected here a note from Paul on how he met Titus in Macedonia and how the good news from Corinth turned the Apostle's anxiety into joy. But he only takes up the matter much later in the letter (7:5-16). First the letter deals at length with the meaning of the apostolic office and the charge laid upon it.

THE APOSTOLIC OFFICE (2:14—6:10)

The whole section 2:14—6:10 interrupts the discussion of the affairs
of the Corinthian church. It is therefore a long digression from the
strict theme of the letter to the Corinthians. Paul bursts out in
thanksgiving for his apostolic office (2:14), and then one word leads
to another, one phrase to another, one thought to another, till this
part of the letter is produced, which again comprises a variety of
different topics and doctrines. From 2:13 and from 7:6, which
again takes up the account of the eventual meeting of Paul and
Titus, we learn how deeply Paul was troubled during his stay in
Troas and Macedonia. The cry of thanks (2:14) may be explained
by the fact that Paul is already thinking (2:13) of the happy story
that he will have to tell in 7:6f. The whole section 2:14—6:10 may
then be said to grow out of the thanksgiving of 2:14.

The Public Nature of the Apostolic Office (2:14—3:3)

A number of statements at the beginning may be summed up as an
affirmation that the apostolic office is visible and active throughout
the whole world. There are Christian communities in some great
cities of the Roman empire. But they are only small groups, and few
know of their existence. The Christian preaching has not reached the
ears of the great and powerful in this world. If they do hear of it,
they do not take it seriously. But the Apostle proclaims the imperious
certainty: the gospel triumphs all over the world. In its acceptance
or rejection the world makes its decision between death and life.

39

NEW TESTAMENT FOR SPIRITUAL READING

The Triumphal March of Christ through the World (2 :14)

[14]*But thanks be to God, who always leads us round in triumph in Christ and makes known through us everywhere the fragrance of his knowledge.*

Paul has spoken of the guidance of God, which he has experienced on the paths of his mission, and of the help of God, which he has had in his service. He has also spoken of the weight of cares, the sadness and distress which were also his lot. These memories cannot hold back the cry of praise which rises from his heart: " Thanks be to God."

The Christian mission is Christ's triumphal march through the world, a procession in which the Apostle too is carried. In a Roman triumph, conquered enemies as well as victorious soldiers made up the train of the general. Either of these elements could be applied to Paul. Christ has conquered his former enemy, and takes him with him as a slave captive to the gospel. Paul often speaks of himself as the slave or servant of Christ (as Rom. 1:1), and will do so later on with particular emphasis when he is in prison (as Eph. 3:1). However, here the Apostle is intent on praising God, and thanking him for the honor bestowed on him. Hence the metaphor should be understood in the sense that God triumphs with Paul and Paul with God. The apostles, " God's fellow workers " (1:24), march along in triumph like the heralds who proclaim the victory or like the soldiers who took part in the battle and now take part in the triumph and are honored along with the conqueror.

The conqueror is God in Christ. For God and through God, Christ gains the victory. In Christ, God is manifest and active in the world. " God has disarmed the principalities and powers and made a spectacle of them in public, triumphing over them through Christ " (Col. 2 : 15).

This beautiful and impressive metaphor is followed by another, which we find very strange. Paul says that the fragrance of the knowledge of God is spread abroad by the apostles. The Old Testament compares good and happy news with sweet odors: " Hearken to me, my pious children . . . send forth fragrance like the storax tree and put forth blossoms like the lily. Send forth your sweet odor and sing your song of praise. Praise the Lord for all his works " (Ecclus. 39 : 13f. [Vg. 39 : 17f.]). The image may also include the notion that the fragrance, understood as a fluid, is a life-giving force, as is water for instance. Plants and animals can live on it if the odor is healthy, but they die if it is poisonous. So too the knowledge of God in Christ sends out a life-giving odor. First it is breath of life to the Apostle, and through him its powerful action is transmitted to others. The Apostle has been given knowledge of God and spreads it abroad in the world through the message of the gospel.

The Good Odor of Christ in the World (2 : 15–16)

[15]*Indeed, we are the fragrance of Christ for God among those who are being saved, as among those who are being lost,* [16a]*to some an odor from death to death, to others an odor from life to life.*

The smell of burning incense does not go unnoticed. Some wrinkle their noses in disgust, others like it. So too, the gospel cannot be ignored by the world. And when the Apostle spreads the good news, like the fragrance of Christ, throughout the world, he touches off very different reactions. The gospel is the point where men decide and divide between death and life. It means life to those who listen to the gospel and accept it. It means judgment and death to the others who reject it. The world divides at the word and grace of God: " The word of the cross is foolishness for those who are being lost; but for us who are being saved, it is the power of God " (1 Cor. 1 : 18).

When the Apostle reveals the word of God to the world, the world is forced to choose, and it makes its decision, undoubtedly, in the free act of human choice. But in this decision a division is also made which is brought about by God. Some are saved and some are lost. " He has mercy on those on whom he wills to have mercy, and he hardens those whom he wills to harden " (Rom. 9 : 18). Nevertheless, Paul affirms with certainty, like the rest of the New Testament, that God's eternal decision is never taken without man also making his own decision.

[16b]*And who is equal to this?*

The preaching of the gospel makes the world decide between life and death. With all this at stake, the question arises : Who is competent to undertake the supreme responsibilities involved in the ministry of preaching?

The Word of God in the World (2 :17)

[17]*We are not, as so many are, pedlars of the word of God, but we act in all sincerity, speaking in Christ as from God and in the sight of God.*

Paul answers the question : Who is equal to this? by speaking at once of how he strives to discharge his office as apostle. He contrasts his way of acting with that of the large number of preachers who treat the word of God like pedlars hawking their wares from door to door. Paul distinguishes himself from false missionaries, who make propaganda for their message in the hope of making money. There must have been many wandering preachers, Greek and Jewish, on the streets and in the squares of the towns, being paid with money for their discourses and their wisdom. At a distance, Paul could have been confused with one of them, though he was in fact completely different. But he is surely thinking rather of certain Christian preachers, from whom he wishes to disassociate himself. The opponents denounced in chapters 10—13 must also be of the same type.

Paul has two main complaints to make about such false preachers. The first is that they trade in the word of God, by making a profit on it, when they look for money, honor, or power. It is a shameful fact that the elders (priests) have to be warned as early as the New Testament, to feed the flock " not in the base hope of gain, but freely and eagerly " (1 Pet. 5:2). To avoid being suspected of hoping to enrich himself by means of the gospel, Paul refuses to accept provision from the communities, though he knows that missionaries have a right to be supported. He earns his keep by manual labor, working on making cloth for tents. So he is able to affirm: " We have not used the gospel as a pretext for enriching ourselves " (1 Thess. 2:5). The other complaint which Paul makes about the false missionaries is that they " adulterate " the gospel, like a cheap jack who hoodwinks the public with inferior, adulterated wares.

In contrast to this trickery, the apostolic ministry, as exercised by Paul and the genuine missionaries, is characterized by four hallmarks, which Paul gives in brief, succinct phrases: in sincerity, from God, in the sight of God, in Christ. Paul can say that he speaks in all sincerity, that is, without cunning, dishonesty, or selfishness; from God, that is, because he proclaims the word of God with a mandate from God; in the sight of God, that is, conscious of his responsibility as God sees, weighs, and judges him; in Christ, that is, in the fellowship of Christ from whom he draws his force.

The Church, the Apostle's Letter of Recommendation (3:1-3)

^{3:1}*Do we begin once more to commend ourselves? Or do we need as some do, letters of recommendation to you, or from you?*

Paul has spoken of how he worked as an apostle in the service of the word of God. Now he fears he may be misunderstood, as though he were producing his credentials, indeed, " commending himself once more." No doubt he had often heard such charges of self-assertion (5:12). He answers his own question to himself with a further one. No doubt Paul's adversaries make their way into the churches bearing letters of introduction from outside, and take away with them similar letters for other churches when they leave. But no one can reproach Paul with having used such means. And just as he had no need of letters of recommendation, so too he has no intention of commending himself. Possibly the Corinthians had allowed themselves to criticize Paul on the basis of the letters of introduction which his opponents produced.

²*You are our letter, inscribed on our heart, known and read by all men.*

Paul needs no recommendations, since he possesses a letter of a very different sort and of immense importance. The letter is the church of Corinth itself, since Paul is known to be its founder and pastor. Here Paul has coined a striking phrase and a vivid metaphor. However, as often in his letters, he does not go on to apply the comparison consistently. He complicates matters by introducing new ideas and other metaphors. The meaning of the original metaphor is clearly brought out when he says: " This letter is known and read by all men." He can proudly say that all the world knows the church in Corinth and recognizes Paul as its apostle. But this metaphor does not fit in well with the subordinate clause: " The letter is written in our heart." If the letter is written in Paul's heart, it can hardly be a public testimony to all men. Nonetheless, it is a phrase which we are glad to read, since Paul uses it to proclaim how dear and precious to him is the church of Corinth. It is more than close to his heart.

[3]*Indeed, you are clearly a letter from Christ, composed through our ministry, written not with ink, but with the Spirit of the living God, not on tablets of stone, but on the tablets of hearts of flesh.*

The metaphor is continued. It was not Paul who wrote the letter. The letter is Christ's, a testimony to his power, because it was Christ, and not the Apostle, who founded the church in Corinth. Christ chose and called the faithful and sanctified the saints, and it is he who will bring them to their final glory. But this, of course, was and is done in the church and through the cooperation of the Apostle. Hence he can say that the letter has been composed through the ministry and the labors of the Apostle.

A letter of this type must be very different from all human writing. There are two great differences which characterize it. It is not written with ink, but through the Spirit of the living God. Wherever the church exists, it has not been produced by human will and effort, but through the creative grace of God. It is always "the church of the living God" (1 Tim. 3:15).

The other characteristic is described in terms reminiscent of the Old Testament. The letter is not on tablets of stone, but on human hearts. Paul is already thinking of the contrast between the old covenant and the new, which he will expound later (3:6f.). On Mount Sinai, the ten commandments were written by the finger of God on stone tablets (Ex. 31:18). But the ancient prophets had already uttered the warning that the commandments had to be inscribed in the heart. Hence Jeremiah says, when speaking of the new covenant: "I will put my law within them and write it on their hearts. I will be their God and they will be my people" (Jer. 31:33). The gospel was inscribed in the hearts of the Corinthians, to make them new men. The church of Corinth thereby became a new creation of God and so the Apostle's great letter of recommendation. Once more we see that Christ, the Spirit, and God are united in the work of redemption (see 1:21f.).

The Old and the New Covenant (3:4-18)

The theme of the contrast between the old and the new covenant was briefly signaled in 3:3. Now it is fully developed. This fits in well with the major theme of the letter, since the glory of the New Testament office and ministry becomes apparent when it is compared with that of the Old Testament.

The Ability to Discharge the Office a Gift of God (3 : 4–5)

⁴But this confidence in God, we have through Christ. ⁵It is not as though we were competent because of our own strength to contemplate anything as coming from ourselves. Our competence is from God . . .

The confidence which the Apostle has of being able to point to the church of Corinth as his letter of recommendation is not self-assurance based on the consciousness of human strength and achievement. It is reliance upon God.

Paul refuses even to attribute to himself the power to contemplate or plan any enterprise, much less to carry it through. All effectiveness comes from God and is given through Christ. Christ himself says: "Without me you can do nothing" (Jn. 15 : 5).

Letter and Spirit (3 : 6–8)

⁶ . . . who has made us competent to be ministers of the new covenant, not that of the letter, but of the Spirit. For the letter kills, but the Spirit gives life.

God has brought about in Christ the time of salvation, and established in him the new testament. It is the work of God. But Paul is the minister and collaborator in God's work, though not through his own strength. God has made him able to cooperate.

The mention of the new covenant is taken from Jeremiah:

" Behold, the days are coming, says the Lord, when I shall establish a new covenant with the house of Israel and the house of Judah . . . Your forefathers violated my covenant, and I rejected them . . . This is the covenant which I will establish with the house of Israel: I will put my law within them and write it in their hearts. I will be their God and they will be my people " (Jer. 31:31-34). This particular prophecy was much quoted in New Testament times. The Jewish theology of the day often cited it and commented on it in the schools. It was in the context of these expectations that the New Testament also had recourse to this prophecy. Jesus himself alludes to it when he speaks at the Last Supper of the shedding of his blood, and calls it the " blood of the testament " (Mk. 14:25). Paul makes it still clearer when he speaks of the " new testament " in 1 Corinthians 11:25, as does Luke 22:20. In the present letter, Paul makes use of the narrative of Exodus about Moses (Ex. 34:29-35) to explain the superiority of the new covenant with regard to the old, and the greater splendor of the new ministry of the apostles with regard to the priestly ministry performed under the Old Testament law. The story in Exodus narrated how Moses had ascended the mountain to receive the law of the ten commandments, which was engraved on tablets of stone. When he came down from the mountain, his face was radiant with divine splendor, so that the Israelites were filled with fear and refused to approach him. Then Moses covered his face with a veil.

In the context of this ancient story, Paul first describes the contrast between the old covenant and the new as the contrast between " letter " (writing) and " Spirit." He calls the old covenant a matter of letters and writing, since it came to Moses in the form of a law inscribed on tablets. In Paul's mind, the stone tablets signify only the written word and the prescriptions and regulations, which are powerless to produce true life. This incompetence beset the old covenant with its imperative laws. It contained many precepts, but did not give strength to fulfill them. The new covenant, on the other hand, was a gift of God which also bestowed the Spirit of God. The Spirit dwelt in the spirit of man, impelling him to action and filling him with joy and strength.

Then Paul continues to develop the contrast between the old covenant and the new, but now in terms of " death " and " life." No one fulfills the law, and no one is able to fulfill it. Nonetheless, to break the law is to be guilty of sin. Indeed, before the holiness and justice of God, the sinner must answer for his sin by death. Ultimately, the harshness of the law as it stands can bring about nothing but death. Hence the old covenant is always doom. But the Spirit who is given in the new covenant is the Spirit who gives life. The new covenant is strength and life, in contrast to the old covenant with its written law, and this is already experienced by the hearers of Jesus. As the gospel of Jesus is preached to them, they feel at once the strength that flows from him and they cry out: " He teaches like one who has power, and not like the doctors of the law " (Mt. 7 : 29).

7But if the ministry of death [whose law was] in letters engraved on stone, was performed in glory, so that the children of Israel could not gaze upon the face of Moses, on account of the glory which shone from it—a glory that was to fade, 8must not the ministry of the Spirit be performed in a much more splendid glory?

Even the old covenant, the covenant of the law, was radiant with glory, as the story of Exodus narrates. The Israelites found that the radiant splendor of Moses' face was too bright to gaze upon. Nonetheless, Paul affirms that such glory was a mere transitory thing. It soon grew dim and disappeared from Moses' face. The radiant glory of God was an outward expression of the sovereign majesty of God. God manifested his glory in the Old Testament through the marvelous deeds which he wrought among his people Israel. The eschatological kingdom of God was to make his glory manifest to all men. But in addition, the New Testament affirms that Christ is to come again in his own and in his Father's glory—and also, that this glory has been and is already made manifest in Christ. Hence, far more brightly than the old covenant, the new covenant, which is the covenant of the Spirit and of life, radiates its glory. The ministry of the apostles, which is to be continued in the priestly ministry of the church, is granted the grace of being able to help to bring about this glory, as it reveals itself permanently and grows steadily through the ages towards its eternal fullness.

Condemnation and Righteousness (3:9–10)

⁹*If the ministry of condemnation was glory, then the ministry of righteousness abounds much more in glory.*

The old and the new covenants are now further contrasted. One is a ministry which brings about condemnation, the other a ministry which brings about righteousness. The old covenant imposes a law which constantly prescribes to men their obligations, but just as constantly convicts them, since they fail to fulfill their obligations. Thus ultimately the law condemns men as guilty. It is true that even under the new covenant men cannot be just and holy in the sight of God by means of their own strength. But if men recognize that they are sinners, God bestows righteousness upon them for the sake of Christ, who died for sin and for the law. Christ made satisfaction for us and opened up to us once more, as our brother, the floodgates of God's grace. This notion is suggested only faintly here. It is fully expounded by Paul in his letter to the Romans (3:21-31). But this is why the new covenant is in fact the covenant which brings about righteousness. Then the same conclusion follows. Since even the old covenant of damnation had its glory, the new covenant of righteousness must have a much more splendid glory. For just as the sinner is deprived of the glory of God, so too the just must possess it.

[10]*Indeed, what was made glorious [in the old covenant] was in this respect not glorified at all, in comparison with the superabundant glory [of the new covenant].*

Here Paul interposes a comment. He has just said that even the old covenant came in glory. But now he adds a restriction. If we compare the old glory with the overwhelming splendor of the new covenant, it will be seen that the former did not really deserve the name of glory. Before the splendor of the new covenant, the brightness of the old fades away into obscurity.

Transition and Truth (3:11)

[11]*If even the transitory was in glory, how much more is that which is permanent full of glory.*

Here is another aspect of the contrast. The old covenant was transitory; the new is eternal. One was provisional, the other the definitive truth. The old covenant came to an end in the new. The new is eternal, and will remain to the end of time. But if even the old and passing covenant had its glory, then the true, new covenant must have a much greater glory.

Veiling and Disclosure (3:12–13)

[12]*Since our hope is so strong, we are bold and frank . . .*

The new covenant radiates glory and bestows righteousness, since they are blessings already within its power. It is true that they are still hidden, and that only faith has certainty of them. But from these present blessings faith draws the hope that it will one day also receive the future and perfected glory. Inspired with this confidence, the Apostle comes forward boldly and frankly. By this Paul means that before men as before God he speaks freely and has no fear. Buoyed up by the certainty of being servant of God, the Christian, like the Apostle, can plead his cause before all men, frankly and fearlessly. But the Christian also has the right and the possibility of speaking freely even to God. As the child of God, he has all the confidence of a child before his father. He can and may pour out his heart frankly (Eph. 3:12; Heb. 4:16). Even now, every day, the Christian may live fearlessly in the sight of God, and one day he will face judgment with the same confidence. Paul too is confident that he can speak out boldly. He displays this confidence in his dealing with men, as he preaches the gospel to them in its fullness, openly and without reserve. He has the same confidence before

God, since he is granted the consoling gift of righteousness and of hope.

¹³ . . . *unlike Moses, who covered his face with a veil, so that the children of Israel should not look upon the end of the transitory* [*glory*].

Finally, the contrast between the old and the new covenant is that of veiling and manifestation. Paul draws this conclusion from the Book of Exodus, which repeats several times that Moses covered his face with a veil. The openness of the Apostle stands out in contrast to Moses. According to the Book of Exodus, Moses hid his face from the people. Paul deduces from this something which is not said expressly in the Old Testament, that Moses did so in order to conceal from the people the disappearance of the fading glory. Paul finds here a proof of the transitory and provisional character of the Old Testament in general.

Paul, on the other hand, needs no concealment. He does not fear that the glory of the New Testament ministry will pass away. For it will last to the end of time. Hence the Apostle can speak freely, march boldly, and face all men openly.

Israel and Church (3:14–18)

¹⁴*But their minds were dulled. For even to the present day this veil remains* [*on the Jews*], *as they hear the books of the old covenant being read to them, and the veil is not taken away, because it is only in Christ that it is done away with.*

Paul sees yet another truth revealed in the story. In any case, the Israelites had failed to see that the splendor on the face of

Moses was fading and passing away. Israel was and remained blind. It did not recognize, and fails to recognize even to the present day, that the whole glory of the old covenant was transitory and has passed away. From Moses to the present day, the day of Christ, Israel has remained equally blind. Just as once a veil covered the face of Moses, so too today a veil covers the Bible of Israel, the book of the old covenant, when it is read to them. This veil conceals from Israel the true knowledge of the Bible. Israel fails to recognize that the Old Testament law as such is no more. It fails to recognize that the Old Testament points to Jesus as the Messiah, that it leads to Christ and finds its goal and end in Christ. Not all Israel's zeal for the law can remove the barrier of the veil, since it is only in Christ that it is done away with.

[15]*Thus, down to the present day, every time Moses is read, a veil remains upon their heart.*

Paul sees a still more profound truth. Having noted the veil first covering the face of Moses, and then masking the Old Testament when it is read, he finally sees it lying on the hearts of the Jews, when they hear the books of Moses read. It is the veil upon their own hearts that prevents them from recognizing the truth. Paul observes the same thing each time: that a veil is interposed between God and the Israelites, so that they do not see and do not understand.

[16]*But whenever one turns to the Lord, the evil is taken away* [Ex. 34:34].

But there is a possibility of the veil being removed and the disaster averted. This too Paul finds already indicated in the story of Moses. The Book of Exodus says that Moses took off the veil whenever he spoke with the Lord. Paul takes this to mean that Israel must turn to the Lord, sincerely and in true faith. Then its blindness will be healed. The veil will be removed from its eyes and from its heart, if it turns to Christ. The history of salvation is understood in the light of faith.

Paul's interpretation of the story of Moses is not that which we usually give it today. But there is no need to think that where he differs from us he must be wrong. The unusual interpretation may well lead us to discover new truths. Paul possibly based his interpretation on what he saw and heard whenever he entered the synagogue. Reverence for the sacred book led the Jews to wrap it in a covering, and they covered their own heads and faces, and wrapped themselves in costly prayer mantles when the sacred text was being read—as the Jews still do at the present day. Paul sees here the painful truth, that the sacred book really remains a closed book to Israel, and that the understanding of Israel is really clouded. The Apostle strove hard and persistently to instruct Israel and to prove to it that its long-awaited Messiah had come in Jesus Christ. But all his efforts were in vain. Sad and profoundly disappointed, Paul recognizes the tragedy of Judaism. Israel truly treasures the sacred scriptures of the Old Testament above all else. It reads the sacred book continually. In its worship, the text is tirelessly expounded. But Israel fails to recognize the true meaning of this book. The Jews revere Moses as the founder of the ancient covenant, but fail to see that Moses testifies to the Messiah who had come in Christ. They fail to see that Moses is trying to lead them to a new covenant. They refuse to recognize the saviour who can strip the bandages from their eyes and lead them to a much greater glory than Moses and the whole ancient covenant possessed.

Yet there is a faint but unmistakable note of hope, to which Paul elsewhere gives more definite expression. He still looks forward to the end of Israel's blindness and the hour of its conversion. There is still the possibility of the people's changing. Israel too is to know the truth and be converted to its Lord Christ. The letter to the Romans speaks of this future day, which is perhaps in the remote distance. " Blindness has come upon part of Israel, until the full number of the gentiles has entered [the church]. Then the whole of Israel too will gain salvation " (Rom. 11 : 25). No one knows when this will be. It is God's sovereign right, to remove the veil and heal Israel's blindness, when he sees that the time for it has come.

[17]*The Lord is the Spirit. But where the Spirit of the Lord is, there is freedom.*

It is to the Lord, Christ, that Israel must be converted. Here Paul adds another remark. This Christ is not merely a personage of past history. He is a living reality here and now. He can work mightily in everyone who turns to him and adheres to him. For in the church and in the world he is present as the Spirit who gives force to the new covenant. Hence to turn to the Lord is to have experience of this living Spirit and to open the heart to him. This therefore is what Israel must do. It must receive and accept this Christ as the Spirit. But Spirit means a new age, and hence also freedom from the yoke of the old law.

Christ is not merely present in the memory of those who think of him, as heroes of the past live on in the admiring and grateful memories of men. And he is not merely present through his words and his teaching; and not merely through the noble or holy example of his commitment and obedience to God. The great figures of humanity are present in this way in our cultural traditions. But Christ is present in every age as the reality, the power and the effectiveness of the Spirit. This is how he is even now the righteousness, the life and the fullness of the church.

But then Christ also means the freedom of the church and of all the faithful in the church. He is freedom from the old law, from sin, and from death. He is freedom for all Christians as well as freedom from the letter. He is also the freedom which resists all efforts to bring faith under human rule, since faith is always directly given to God and lives immediately in the sight of God. This affirmation of freedom in the church should not be misunderstood. Freedom does not mean casting off all restraints. The freedom which Paul preached was already misunderstood in this way. His answer was that freedom does not mean freedom from the law of God, but freedom for God and for the service of the neighbor (Rom. 6:1, 15, 22). Nonetheless, it would be wrong to cease to preach freedom in the church. There is a virtue of freedom, which faith must be bold enough to practice. It is exercised when it is no longer the external precept which is decisive, but the inward dedication. What matters then is not the service of the lips, but the prayer of the heart; not reliance on one's own work, but confidence in the generous love of God.

[18]*But we all gaze upon the glory of the Lord, as though in a mirror, but still with eyes unveiled, and we are changed into the same image from glory to glory, this being wrought by the Lord who is Spirit.*

Paul comes to the end of his train of thought, which he here enlarges and brings to a climax. He depicts what has happened and is happening to the church, in contrast to the blindness of

Israel. The church's visage is not covered by a veil. It can contemplate the bright majesty of God with eyes unveiled. God's glory is revealed in its sight, and the church can bear it, without being blinded as Israel was. For the church, God is a gracious God. But it is also true that God remains the great mystery even for his elect. The church cannot know God as he is in his own most intrinsic life and nature. It can only reflect his image as though in a mirror and it can only see him in this mirror. God is invisible, and he can be grasped and known only in images.

But knowledge of God is never confined to the fact that men take cognizance of him. The living God is active and powerfully efficacious in this knowledge. And hence the church is changed into the likeness of the image of God which is before its eyes. The transformation is not total and immediate. It takes place gradually, always coming closer to this goal. The traces of sin and death are wiped away. The sonship of God which was Jesus' own is imparted to believers. And this is all brought about by the Lord Christ who is present in the world and the church as the all-powerful Spirit. The process will be brought to its completion when—as Paul undoubtedly means—at the second coming of Christ the living and the dead will be transformed in the general resurrection and taken up into the glory of God.

Paul again and again speaks in similar terms, in order to describe the future which he pictured as close at hand. Thus he says: " We await the coming of the Lord Jesus Christ from heaven, who will change our lowly bodies and make them like his own glorious body, through the power which he has to subject all things to his sway " (Phil. 3:21); or again: " As we have borne the image of the earthly Adam, so too we shall bear the image of Christ as the heavenly Adam . . . We shall not all sleep, but we shall all be changed " (1 Cor. 15:49–51).

The Light in the World (4:1–6)

Using a number of metaphors and a rich vocabulary, Paul now describes the office of the apostle as the light of God in the darkness of the world. He speaks once more of his main interest, which is to defend his office and his conduct of it against suspicions and attacks in Corinth (4:2.5), as he had done again and again in chapters 2 and 3.

Preaching without Deceit (4: 1–2)

⁴:¹*Therefore, because we have this ministry, as we have been shown mercy, we do not lose heart.*

Paul affirms once more that what constitutes the apostle is not his own merits and abilities, but the mercy of God, shown both in the call and in the bestowal of the powers to carry out the work. With this truth in mind, he is far from all arrogance and self-assurance. But since he also knows that what counts is not the human effort but the power of God, he remains tireless and does not lose heart, even in face of the opposition which he has to overcome at Corinth.

²*We have discarded everything underhand and disgraceful; we do not go about practicing deceit or falsifying the word of God. We preach the truth openly, and thus present ourselves to all men's conscience, in the sight of God.*

Paul knows that his conscience is clear. He has nothing secret and wrong to be ashamed of. What does he mean by " secret and shameful things "? He is probably thinking of the suspicions

and reproaches which he has already defended himself against:
" Our words of exhortation do not spring from deceit or wrong
intentions, and contain no trickery . . . Nor has there been any
attempt to flatter, nor have we sought pretexts to enrich ourselves " (1 Thess. 2 : 3–5). Hence Paul is thinking of the charges
of greed which have been brought against him (12 : 7f.), of
cunningness in his procedures (1 : 13f.), of distortion of the word
of God (2 : 17). Nonetheless, he knows that he is carrying out
honestly the work of an apostle, since he proclaims the truth
of the gospel with regard to God's designs and works. If the
gospel is not everywhere listened to and accepted, his preaching
is not at fault. Having already affirmed that he speaks freely and
frankly (3 : 12), he now repeats that his conscience is clear before
men and God.

Blindness of Unbelief (4:3–4a)

³*But if our gospel is veiled, it is only veiled for those who are
on the path of perdition, ⁴ᵃfor the unbelievers, whose minds have
been blinded by the god of this present world . . .*

Paul defends himself in particular against the reproach that his
preaching is mystifying and unintelligible, and leaves important
matters in obscurity. Such charges were undoubtedly brought
against Paul. On what grounds we do not know. However, he
admits that a veil is drawn upon his gospel, though only hiding
it from the unbelievers who are on the way to eternal loss. It is
true that the bright radiance of the gospel does not shine for
those whose minds have been blinded by Satan, so that they
cannot see the light of the gospel, but remain in the darkness
of unbelief.

Brightness of Faith (4:4b–6)

⁴ᵇ. . . *so that they do not see the light shining from the gospel of the glory of Christ, who is the image of God.*

The gospel has a radiant splendor. This it receives from the splendor of Christ, and this in turn stems from the fact that he is the image of God. When he uses the word " image," Paul means something quite different from what our ordinary use of the term suggests. We use " image " to speak, for instance, of the picture of someone who remains absent, the picture or photograph serving to remind us of the original on account of the likeness which the image contains. But when Paul speaks of " image," he means that the original or prototype actually becomes visible and manifest. Hence Christ can be termed " the image of the invisible God, the first-born before all creation " (Col. 1:15). The term does not mean simply a faint similarity. Paul uses it as a doctrinal formula and a profession of faith. It does not mean that Christ is merely like God and only a reflection of him. Paul is professing his faith and the faith of the church, which is that in Christ the eternal God has manifested himself and entered the world. Christ is God as he appears outwardly. He is the manifestation or epiphany of God in the world. It is the same truth which is expressed by Christ in the Gospel of St. John: " He who sees me, sees the Father " (Jn. 14:9.)

⁵*For we do not preach our own person. It is Christ Jesus the Lord whom we proclaim, and ourselves as your servants for the sake of Jesus.*

Paul now returns to the defense of his ministry. He proclaims

Christ, not himself. For the one thing which he always preaches is that Christ is the Lord. The profession of faith, " Christ is the Lord," means that Jesus the Messiah who has been raised from the dead and taken up into the glory of God now reigns as Lord over the church and the world. It was a formula which gave in the briefest possible compass the primitive Christian confession of faith. But in this same preaching, Paul also acknowledges Christ as his own Lord and himself as the servant of this master. Hence it is impossible that Paul should proclaim himself. It is always the Lordship of Christ which is proclaimed. As the servant of Christ, Paul, for the sake of his master, is also servant of others, including the church of Corinth. Christ too had been the servant of all. Thus he could say of himself: " The Son of man has not come to be served, but to serve, and to give his life as a ransom for the many " (Mk. 10:45). Paul appeals to this example given by Christ when he writes: " Do not think merely of your own interests. Let each one think of the other. Let this be your mind, as it was the mind of Christ Jesus . . . who humbled himself, obedient unto death, the death of the cross " (Phil. 2:4–8). He who serves such a Lord cannot but be the servant of all.

⁶For God who said: " Let there be light from darkness," has illumined our hearts with the brilliant light of the knowledge of the glory of God on the face of Christ.

Paul has already affirmed that the glory of Christ is the embodiment of the glory of God (4:4). Now he takes in the whole vast range of history and the history of salvation to affirm that God is the source of all light and all glory in the world. It was God who created light at the beginning, as the first chapter of Genesis

relates: " He said, ' Let there be light '; and there was light "
(Gen. 1:3). It is the same God who shines forth once more from
the face of Christ, through whom he reveals himself to the world.
And he shines forth again and again in the hearts of those who
believe. Possibly Paul is here thinking of the moment of his
conversion on the road to Damascus, when the Jesus whom he
was persecuting revealed himself as the Christ of glory. But his
statement goes beyond this to speak of faith in general. The
brightness and splendor of faith are always brought about by the
bright light of God which radiates from the visage of Christ.
From the beginning, God is always the creator who makes light
shine in darkness, since God is light. This same God manifests
himself again and again in the course of history in similar actions
and words, gestures, and symbols. So too the Gospel of St. John
says that Christ, as the light of God, was always in the world, but
that now he has been fully manifested (Jn. 1:4.5.9). In such
statements as those of 4:4 and 4:6, Paul endeavors to explain
the origins of belief and unbelief. And he affirms that neither
faith nor refusal of faith is simply man's decision. If man in his
unbelief disregards God, he may indeed imagine that he does so
simply by virtue of his own decision. But Paul affirms that man's
enemy, Satan, has blinded the unbeliever (4:4). On the other
hand, if a man comes to believe, he has no occasion to boast.
God brings about faith in the heart, through his light (4:6).
Nonetheless, Paul affirms equally strongly that in the act of faith
or the refusal of faith, man's own decision also comes into play.
Paul speaks several times of the " obedience of faith " (Rom.
1:5). In the act of faith, man listens to God and obeys his command, while unbelief refuses to listen and obey. These seemingly
contradictory statements about the action of God and of man
occur quite frequently in Paul. It may be difficult to reconcile

them logically. But faith recognizes that they describe the reality of the cooperation of God and man, where God is sovereign Lord and man is his obedient servant—and friend.

Between Life and Death (4:7–18)

A new train of thought begins at 4:7 and goes on to 5:10. Paul continues to describe the office of the apostle, but now he shows how life and death, time and eternity, are linked together in the life and the office of the apostle. The first part of the exposition (4:7–18) shows the life of the apostle as a passage through death into life. In the most intimate fellowship of life and suffering, the disciple follows his master through the Passion into glory. This burden of suffering releases in the present time the forces of patience and steadfastness, of hope and the assurance of eternal salvation.

The Apostle and the Life and Death of Jesus (4:7–13)

⁷But we have this treasure in earthenware vessels, so that the immense power may be seen to be the power of God and not ours.

Paul has depicted glory as the characteristic of the office of the apostle. But reality seems to tell a very different story. The reality seems to be suffering, persecution and humiliation. Paul himself observes the contrast. But others, Jews and Greeks, and even the Corinthians, will find the contrast much more blatant than he does. So he now tries to explain the apparent contradiction.

Undoubtedly, the apostolic office is a treasure of inestimable value. But the treasure is kept in an earthenware vessel. The metaphor has two points. One is that the treasure is kept in an unimpressive container which does not suggest that there is anything precious hidden within. Those who only see the earthenware vessel have no idea of the treasure. The other point is that an earthenware vessel is easily broken. It has to be handled very carefully. If the vessel breaks, the treasure is scattered and left without protection. Hence the apostle must bear in mind that a very precious treasure has been committed to his care when he was called, and that it needs to be guarded with painstaking loyalty. The metaphor also applies to all disciples of Christ. The " outward " man who must undergo suffering and death contains a treasure of supreme value—the spiritual life and being of the " inward " man, the grace of salvation which is a treasure of inestimable value.

Paul explains the meaning of the contrast between the vessel and its contents. If the apostle were a man who made an impression by his outward gifts and actions, his achievements might be ascribed to his own efforts, and God's work in him might go unnoticed and without acknowledgement. Hence God makes weak men the vessels of his grace, so that their power may be recognized as the power of God, as coming from God, and not confused with human abilities. Thus the power of the apostle is seen to be God's immense power. God's power is immense, since it surpasses everything that men are accustomed to. The apostle, like all other Christians, lives a life which has always two aspects: his own deficiency and the supremely powerful help of God.

[8]*We are always afflicted, but never crushed, at a loss but never despairing,* [9]*persecuted but not abandoned, brought low but not destroyed.*

In verses 8–12 human weakness and divine power are contrasted
several times, at first in brief phrases, and then in longer sentences. The first term in each case designates the grievous suffering which the apostle must bear. The second member affirms
again and again that the apostle is never crushed, which is the
great proof of God's power. This is the continually new miracle
which faith experiences.

The apostle—and believers in general—will be persecuted by
enemies, but will never be abandoned by the divine helper. Possibly the persecutor overtakes his victim and dashes him brutally
to the ground. But, as though by a miracle, he is prevented from
striking the death blow.

[10]*At all times, we bear about in our bodies the death of Jesus,
so that the life of Jesus may also be made manifest in our bodies.*

The contrasts hitherto were all formulated in general terms
which could apply to all men. Now they appear as those which
are intrinsic to the life of Christian faith. Paul knows that he
is delivered over to an unending process of dying, by which he
means the continual dangers and deprivations, the bodily and
mental burdens which threaten to crush him. He is perpetually
in his death throes. He understands why this must be so when
he thinks of the destiny of Jesus. Jesus went through death to
life. Just as the apostle preaches the Passion of Jesus, so too he
must embody it and reënact it in his life. Nonetheless, in the
direst and most deadly tribulation, the great transformation takes
place, as it did in the life story of Jesus. Jesus passed through
death to the new life which he attained in the resurrection and
in his exaltation to the right hand of the Father.

The apostle too experiences this life after his own passion.

He experiences it as the power which overcomes all suffering and preserves the life of the body from destruction. But at the same time, and still more strongly, he experiences it as the mental and spiritual power which is undefeated and vigorous in face of all suffering. This present life of power will be perfected in the future life of eternity (4:14). Paul returns again and again to life and death as the law of Christian being: " If we suffer with him, we shall also be glorified with him " (Rom. 8:17), or: " To know him and the power of his resurrection and the fellowship of his sufferings " (Phil. 3:10). These sentences are, as it were, the response to the word of the Lord: " If any one will come after me, he must renounce himself, take up his cross and follow me " (Mk. 8:34).

[11]For we who live are being continually delivered over to death for the sake of Jesus, so that the life of Jesus also may be made manifest in our mortal bodies.

Life and death, death and life do not merely succeed one another. They both take place at one and the same time in each Christian believer. Thus Christ is the principle and model of life in the disciple, since both Christ and the disciple share the one fellowship of suffering and life.

Paul speaks again and again of this fellowship of death and life with Christ, especially in the great chapter dealing with baptism in the letter to the Romans. There he says: " We have been baptized into the death of Christ . . . As Christ was raised from the dead through the glorious power of the Father, so too we must let our conduct be inspired by the newness of life . . . As we have been made one with him in the likeness of his death, so too shall we be at one with him in the resurrection " (see

Rom. 6:3–11). Here the death and life of Christ are not merely an example held up to our imitation in our moral life. They are also the prototype, the original as it were, which is reproduced and recreated in Christians through the efficacy of the sacrament. They are reënacted in the Christian's baptism, and he must verify and realize them in his whole life. Here in 2 Corinthians 4, Paul does not speak explicitly of this dying and rising in the sacrament. But for Paul, life and sacrament are indissolubly linked. Thus the doctrine of baptism in the letter to the Romans (ch. 6) forms a unity with the doctrine of life in the Second Epistle to the Corinthians (ch. 4), as they must form a unity in the life of every Christian.

[12]*Thus death is at work in us, but life in you.*

Paul closes this train of thought with a surprisingly new idea. He sums up by repeating that death is doing its work in him. But he does not go on to say that hence too life is at work in him. He says instead that life is doing its work " in you." This life is the spiritual and doctrinal riches of the community at Corinth and, in addition, the life of the whole church. By this Paul does not merely mean that the community is being built up by means of the preaching and labors of the Apostle. What he affirms is also that there is a profound relationship between vicarious or substitutional dedication and salvation, whereby the death of one means life for another. Here the Apostle expresses his conviction that he is not merely the teacher, ruler, and father of the community, but also its priest and mediator. He knows that he is sacrificing himself on behalf of the church, and that from his sacrifice life will come. The Apostle's self-dedication bears fruit in the church: " If the grain of wheat does not fall into the earth and die, it remains alone. But if it dies, it brings forth much fruit (Jn. 12:24f.).

¹³*But since we have the same Spirit of faith, of which it is written: " I have believed, therefore have I spoken " [Ps. 116: 10], we too believe, and therefore we too speak.*

Paul has spoken unreservedly of his distress and afflictions. He can speak of all these daily experiences of weakness because he speaks in faith. Hence this sense of his weakness does not oppress him. He is inspired by the same strong Spirit of faith which moved the psalmist to pray, after his rescue from mortal danger: " I believed, therefore I can speak in praise of God " (Ps. 116:10). This will always be the utterance of faith, as it experiences the wonderful might of God. Man, however, cannot simply decide to believe of his own accord. Faith is the work of the Spirit, an action of God upon man (4:6).

The Church and the Life and Death of Jesus (4:14–15)

¹⁴*For we know that he who raised up Jesus will also raise us up with Jesus, and bring us into his own presence along with you.*

The power which enables Paul to speak and work in spite of all his tribulations is faith in the risen Lord. For the resurrection of Christ is the pledge of the resurrection, the life of the risen Lord the source of the indefectible life of the church. The eternal God who did not abandon Christ to death will see to it that no faith is in vain and he will not leave life under the sway of death. Paul affirms this again and again in his preaching on the resurrection: " He who raised Christ Jesus from the dead will also give life to our mortal bodies " (Rom. 8:11), or: " Christ has been raised from the dead as the first-fruits of those who have slept " (1 Cor. 15:20).

After the resurrection, those raised from the dead will be presented before the throne of God, not indeed for judgment, but for the truest of triumphs: " He has reconciled you in his earthly life by his death, in order to present you holy, pure, and spotless before God " (Col. 1:22). Paul begins by speaking of himself. But he cannot speak of his hope of eternal life without including his community. Even in eternal life, the Apostle and his church are together. His way of speaking suggests that he takes it for granted, without more ado, that this personal fellowship begun on earth will persist also in heaven. Thus Paul is certain that there is such a thing as " personal immortality," where we see one another again.

[15]*All is for your sakes, so that grace may increase as more and more are won and inspire immense thankfulness to the glory of God.*

The Apostle and the community form a unity. All that the Apostle plans and executes and suffers takes place for the sake of his readers, for the sake of the church. But the church is not the ultimate end and goal. The end of all things is that God be honored and glorified. The divine grace which calls men to believe and converts their hearts to God will extend wider and wider as more men come to faith. But the more believers there are, the more prayer and thanksgiving are poured out to God. The ultimate end of all preaching and missionary work is that a mighty chorus of praise may go up from earth to heaven (see 1:11; 9:12).

Time and Eternity (4:16-18)

[16]*Therefore we do not lose heart, and though our outward man is perishing, our inward man is renewed day by day.*

Paul takes up once more the assertions he has just made (4:7-12) and rounds them off with some weighty remarks which are couched in a very pregnant style. The " outward man," that is, the bodily and perishable part of man, may well be worn out and his vital energies exhausted. But the " inward man," that is, the spiritual and imperishable part of man, who in the Christian view of things is man living by faith and the Spirit—the Christ coming to be in the Christian—is created anew each day by God's power and love. This inward man is " the new man, renewed according to the image of the creator " (Col. 3:10), " the new creation " itself (2 Cor. 5:17).

[17]*The slight tribulation of the present time produces for us an eternal weight of glory, in superabundant measure, a superabundant yield . . .*

The deliverance which faith now experiences day by day will also appear as the future, definitive salvation on the last day. The tribulation of the present moment is slight in comparison with the glory that is to come. " The sufferings of the present time are not worthy of consideration compared to the future glory which will be revealed in us " (Rom. 8:18). Glory grows out of distress. This does not mean that the sufferer and the martyr can merit for themselves their eternal reward. No one insists as earnestly as Paul that righteousness and above all glory are always a gift and a grace (Rom. 3:24-28; Eph. 2:8). But the truth is that God's grace has so ordained matters that dying produces life.

[18]. . . *for we do not look to the visible, but to that which is unseen. For that which is visible passes away, while the invisible is eternal.*

The world of eternity to which the eyes of faith are turned is not a visible thing. Hence the Christian does not fix his gaze on the visible, but on what is invisible—as the text concludes, in a deliberately paradoxical formulation. The fact that they cannot be seen does not diminish the value of the eternal blessings; if rightly understood, it rather enhances them. For the visible is perishable while the invisible is eternal. Hence faith is not content with what is seen. It looks out for what is unseen. Elsewhere too (Phil. 3 : 8–16) Paul speaks with deep feeling and in moving terms of faith and love as they are ordained to their eternally abiding goal. And the letter to the Hebrews speaks of faith in similar terms: " Faith is the assurance of what is hoped for, the conviction of what is unseen " (Heb. 11 : 1).

The Heavenly Homeland (5:1–10)

When speaking of daily death (4 : 7–18), Paul also affirmed his certainty of unending life (4 : 14.18). This links up with 5 : 1–10, where Paul expounds more fully the theme of the final hopes. But the one theme is treated very differently in the two sections. In 4 : 7–18, Paul speaks of life and death in terms of the inward personal experience of them which is given in faith and holiness. In 5 : 1–10, he describes the last things in statements of faith and doctrine, as though he were speaking of entirely future events. Having just said that in the present daily dying his union with the Lord only grows stronger and stronger (4:11.16), he now goes on to say that life in the body means separation from the Lord (5:6–10). In the previous section Paul proclaimed his confidence that the conquest of death was already certain, indeed, already accomplished (4:16f.), in the next section he speaks anxiously of death yet to be overcome (5:2–5). It can hardly be said that Paul has unconsciously contradicted himself in a short space of time in so closely woven a discourse. But it must be admitted that the same subject can suggest to Paul very different aspects from which he can draw very different types of doctrine. This strange juxtaposition in the text may serve to remind us that the letters of the Apostle are not like catechisms and textbooks which enumerate the truths of faith in systematic order. As we study the text we must always ask what Paul really and ultimately means to say to the reader or hearer in each case, how he is trying to challenge him, and in what direction he wishes to impel him.

In the Earthly Tent (5:1–4)

^{5:1}*We know that when the earthly tent of our house is demolished, we receive a building from God, an eternal house not made with hands, in heaven.*

Paul compares the earthly body with a tent, such as the Bedouin live in. When it is time for the nomad to move on, the tent is taken down. So too the tent in which man dwells, his body, is pulled down when the time of his stay is ended with death.

Death can also be described as transfer into another house. But here in our text it is not said that this new house is heaven. No doubt the New Testament speaks of heaven as an eternal dwelling-place, as when, for instance, there are said to be many places in the house of the Father (Jn. 14:2), or when Christians are said to be on the way to the heavenly Jerusalem (Heb. 12:22). But in the present text the new house is a new bodily frame for the spirit. This new body is "received from God": it is of heavenly origin, and hence it partakes of the properties of the divine realm. There is nothing earthly and perishable about it. It is not made by human hands or by human effort. Like all heavenly things, this body exists from eternity in heaven. This heavenly house which is already preëxisting in heaven, will be given us at the hour of death.

There is a certain amount of obscurity attaching to these words of Paul, but clearly his final expectation is hope of a new body which is the gift of God, and hope of a transformation of the perishable into the imperishable which only God can bring about. And since God is free in his actions, he is also free to bestow the heavenly body in whatever form he wills. All words that can be uttered about it are only metaphors drawn from human understanding. God alone knows what the reality will be.

²As long as we are in this [tent] we do indeed sigh, longing to be clothed still further with our dwelling-place from heaven, ³in the hope that when we have put it on we shall not be found naked.

Those who know of the new body and live in hope of it are spurred on by longing for it. For it is not earthly and imperfect like the present one. It will be heavenly and perfect.

But Paul changes the metaphor. Instead of the new house into which we enter, he speaks of new clothing which we are to put on. Since in death man loses his former type of body, he is naked till he has received his new bodily form. He longs to receive the new garment in order not to find himself naked. It would indeed

be our wish—as Paul explains human yearning for fulfillment—
to put on the new garment over the present one, without first
being stripped of the old. For we dread to find ourselves naked.
Since laying aside the garment means dying, and being naked
obviously indicates an intermediate state, it would be our wish,
Paul explains, that the present earthly body should be given the
covering of the heavenly one, without the painful process of
being stripped, that is, without our dying.

⁴*We who are in this tent feel oppressed and sigh, because we do
not wish to be stripped but to be further clothed [with the
heavenly tent], in order that what is mortal may be absorbed by
life.*

Though the terms and metaphors which Paul uses are somewhat
strange, we understand what he means. He feels that death is an
adversary under whose violence men succumb. Death is the
enemy who remains to the end: " The last enemy to be destroyed
is death " (1 Cor. 15:26). Here Paul expresses a truth which all
men recognize. Death is not the friend of man. Since it is the
destroyer of life it is always felt to be the enemy. It is the profound longing of man never to part with his life, but to gain a
new and eternal life in addition to it, before he loses his earthly
life. His longing is that what is mortal should not have to die,
but instead go through a transformation which will deliver it and
open the way to life.

At Home with the Lord (5:5-10)

⁵*But he who has prepared us for this is God, who has also given
us the pledge of the Spirit.*

Man is tossed about by perpetual fears and hopes in face of death. Paul's answer is to offer the certainty of faith. God has created man for this very end: to be given this further covering. The creative work of God is always directed by a purpose, and what he plans he carries out to the end. This plan too he will bring to fulfillment, and the pledge and guarantee of the final state is the gift of the Spirit which is already bestowed. Once more, as in 1:22, the Spirit is described as the initial stage of the fullness of the gifts to come. The Spirit raises man above the earthly and sinful. He spiritualizes the body and the nature of man. The full perfection of this present gift of the Spirit will be when man one day receives the bodily form which corresponds to the divine Spirit bestowed upon him.

So we are always encouraged, and we know that as long as we are present to the body, we are absent from the Lord.

Here Paul takes up new metaphors. Life on earth means to be far away from the Lord Christ, in a foreign country. Death means to go home to the Lord. The risen Christ was exalted into heaven. As heavenly Lord, he is now in a totally different sphere of being, which is also the other and the permanent home of the Christian, towards which he is traveling. On earth the Christian is in a foreign land, waiting for the moment of his departure when he will go to his Lord.

We walk in faith and not by vision.

Paul often speaks in such a way as to affirm that to be a Christian already means to be with Christ or in Christ even at the present moment (2:14; 13:4). Nonetheless, the Christian's existence with

Christ at present is always only the life which is lived in faith. He will only be fully with the Lord when he lives by vision. "We see now in a mirror obscurely, but then face to face" (I Cor. 13:12).

⁸But still we take courage, and would wish rather to be exiled from the body and be at home with the Lord.

The Apostle—and each Christian—desires to go out of the body and be at home with the Lord. In 5:3 Paul spoke of the dread of death, which he explained as dread of being naked in an intermediate state. Here this very natural dread seems to be overcome in the confident knowledge that death means going to the Lord. Fellowship with the Lord will remain even in dying, and this is what conquers all the terrors of death. It is the same confidence of which Paul assures the Thessalonians. Many things remain uncertain and secret as regards death, but there Paul's final exhortation to his Christians is: "We shall be for ever with the Lord. Console each other with these words" (I Thess. 4:17f.).

⁹Hence our one ambition is to be pleasing to him, whether we are in exile or whether we are at home.

Christian hope is not an empty fantasy. It is a formative influence in Christian life, indeed in the everyday life of the Christian. The life of the Christian must always be directed by the effort to be pleasing to the Lord. The Christian may only hope to dwell one day in heaven with the Lord, if he is pleasing to him now. Only if he is acceptable to the Lord at present will his departure from the body mean going home to the Lord. Otherwise it would mean falling under judgment.

¹⁰For we must all be made manifest before the judgment seat of Christ, so that each may receive the reward for what he has done in the body, be it good or evil.

It is of decisive importance to be found pleasing to the Lord. For the verdict passed on us at judgment will depend on this. Judgment means being laid bare or manifest before the judgment seat of Christ. The judge in the great universal judgment, according to the faith of the Old Testament, is God the Lord. Indeed, he proves himself to be Lord by being judge. The New Testament holds fast to this conviction: " God will judge the world " (Rom. 3 : 6). But in the New Testament Christ is named as judge as well as God. Jesus, who calls himself the Son of man, says of this Son of man that he will come again as judge of the world (Mt. 25 : 31). Then God will " pass judgment through Christ Jesus " (Rom. 2 : 16). In our present text Christ appears in fact as the universal judge. In the Gospel of St. John we actually read that " the Father judges no one, but has given all judgment to the Son " (Jn. 5 : 22).

At judgment man will receive the reward due to him, according to what he has done, good or evil. That judgment is passed according to men's works is as evident a truth for Paul as the other truth which he particularly emphasizes, that man can never merit righteousness through works, since it is always a gift of God to man. " We are justified gratuitously by his grace " (Rom. 3 : 24). The work of God and the work of man are closely linked. God accomplishes the great work of salvation, but this does not mean that man may remain idle. The gift of God is a charge and a duty laid upon men. And hence Paul urges insistently: " Work out your salvation in fear and trembling. For it is God who is at work in you " (Phil. 2 : 12f.). Man may never forget that God is his partner in the work of salvation. This partnership will be his perdition if he forgets it. Hence the message of grace does not release men from the duty of moral action, it is rather the first real summons thereto.

The Reconciliation between God and the World
(5:11—6:2)

Paul returns once more to the theme which recurs again and again in the second letter to the Corinthians, the defense of his apostolic ministry, using it as the occasion to develop the theology of the sacred office in the church. In this new section he considers the office under the aspect of a ministry of reconciliation. It brings into the world and bestows on the world the benefits of the reconciliation with God which Christ has brought about (5:18–20). The doctrine of Christ's work of salvation is also profoundly treated.

The Zeal of the Apostle (5:11–13)

[11]We know therefore what it is to fear the Lord, and it is with this in mind that we seek to persuade men. Before God we are fully manifest. And I hope that we are also fully manifest to your conscience.

The Apostle too will have to answer for his life in the coming judgment (5:10). Hence fear of the Lord is the basis of his service and directs its course, whether he thinks of man or God. And hence he strives to convince men by his preaching and to win them over. But before God, under whose watchful eye he knows he always lives, Paul's whole life lies open. Hence he cannot but perform his ministry in sincerity and purity. He hopes that the Corinthians, if they question their consciences sincerely, will see and acknowledge the honesty and integrity of the Apostle.

[12]*We do not commend ourselves to you once more, but we give you an opportunity to take pride in us, so that you may have something [to say] for those who take pride in outward appearances, but not in [sincerity of] heart.*

Paul seems to hear once more (see 3:1) the reproach that he is recommending himself. He rejects the charge. But it remains true that the Corinthians should commend him and Paul wishes to give them the chance of doing so. The church of Corinth should take pride in him as their apostle. They should celebrate the fact and so proclaim that they have no intention of being separated from him. This is something that the Corinthians should do when dealing with people—adversaries of Paul, obviously—who do in fact gladly commend themselves. But they take pride in outward show, in the things that meet the eye, but which are without intrinsic value. What they boast of, as may be deduced from what follows, is perhaps their Jewish ancestry and their observation of the law, or their relationships with the first apostles or possibly also their gift of eloquence. But they cannot take pride in any inward worth of their hearts. By the latter Paul means such qualities as honesty, unselfishness, union with Christ, and the gift of the Spirit.

[13]*If we have been carried away, it was for God; if we are circumspect, it is for you.*

It appears that his opponents have also belittled Paul by saying that he was often beside himself or out of his senses. The charge may have been occasioned by his religious enthusiasm which knew no ordinary bounds, or by his missionary zeal which knew no rest. Or again, it may have been a wrong interpretation of his marvelous charismatic gifts, such as his visions and ecstasies. Paul does not deny the existence of such experiences and gifts. But if he was ever out of his senses, it was for God. It was from God that he received these extraordinary gifts; they belonged to God, and he served God with them. Hence he commits all this to the judgment of God. But Paul was not always beside himself. Far more often, he has been fully self-possessed. He is not merely an ecstatic who belongs to God and to himself and otherwise has little care for the things about him. He is also a man of clear and circumspect insight and action, thereby ceaselessly serving the church, in particular the church of Corinth. In ecstasy or in sobriety, Paul will never serve his own interests or commend himself. His life does not belong to him but to God and the church.

Christ's Work of Reconciliation (5 : 14–17)

¹⁴*The love of Christ constrains us, since we are convinced that one died for all. Hence all are dead.*

If the Apostle appears restless and immoderate, it is because another power has possession of him. The love of Christ, that is, Christ, has seized him lovingly, holds him fast, and urges him on. In the same sense he also says: " I live in the faith of the Son of God, who loved me and delivered himself up for me " (Gal. 2 : 20).

The overwhelming revelation of this love of Christ was that he, the one, died for all. This " for " can mean that he gave his life for the sake of mankind and for their salvation : " His blood poured out for the many " (Mk. 14:25). But the " for " may also indicate vicarious satisfaction, in the sense that he died instead of those who should have paid the penalty of death. Paul thinks of Christ dying on the cross and making expiation for the transgressions of men against the law when he says : " Christ has ransomed us from the curse of the law, by becoming a curse for us " (Gal. 3:13). In our present text also the " for " means " instead of."

Since Christ has died for all and in the place of all, all are dead. Christ on the cross incorporated all men within himself and represented all. Hence the death of Christ is also the death of all mankind. In Christ, the verdict of God's judgment was pronounced upon all, as upon sinners who were lost, and in his death, judgment was executed upon all. All men can truly say : " I am crucified along with Christ " (Gal. 2:19).

[15]*And he died for all, so that those who live should no longer live for themselves but for him who for them died and was raised from the dead.*

Christ was raised from the dead. Fellowship with him in death also procures the fellowship of life. Through Christ's being raised from the dead, we also live. " If we have died with Christ, we believe that we shall also live with him " (Rom. 6:8). But those who have been established in a new life may no longer live for their own interests. They must put their whole life at the service of him who died for them and rose again. Just as Christ lived for others, so too Christians must live for others. The life of

Christ on which their life is modeled always claims and lays
obligations on their life. " None of us lives for himself, and none
dies for himself. Whether we live or die, we belong to the Lord "
(Rom. 14:7f.).

*16"Hence from now on we know nobody according to the flesh.
And if we also knew Christ according to the flesh, now we no
longer know him so.*

Paul draws further conclusions from the fundamental principle
that all are dead. The former life is over and done with for all.
Hence Paul can no longer pass judgment upon anyone according
to the flesh. Here flesh does not mean sin, but the transitory
things of earth, in all their ramifications, such as ancestry, rank,
standing among men, history, and possessions. All this means
nothing now.

This is true even with regard to Christ. Paul is undoubtedly
thinking of his adversaries, who maintained that Paul's apostolic
office was inferior to that of the twelve apostles who had been
personally chosen by Jesus during his life on earth, while Paul
had only been called by the risen and exalted Lord on the way to
Damascus. Paul also had to defend himself against such efforts to
belittle him in the letter to the Galatians (1:11–17). It is in this
context that he now affirms that all relationships to the earthly
Jesus are now unimportant. They bestow no privileges and pre-
cedence. The appeal to such relationships is valueless compared
to the fact of belonging to the exalted Christ, who works in the
church as the Spirit (3:17).

*17He who is in Christ is a new creation. The old has passed
away. A new world has come to be.*

In the death of Christ all have died. But from the death of Christ new life came forth. And those who have died with Christ, that is to say, Christians, partake of this life. The church is a new creation. Christians are new men. The old world and the old age, with their misery, sin, and enmity to God, have been swept away. The renewal of the world which God had promised and which all had awaited with so much longing, is now a reality.

But can this be maintained in view of the reality which meets the eye, where failure, fault, and sin continue to exist? And does not Paul himself often speak in different terms? Does he not say that " this world which we see is passing away " (1 Cor. 7:31)? Thus the world is only to pass away at the future consummation of all things. Up to the present, it continues to exist very really as the old world. Death still reigns, and he will only be destroyed as the very " last enemy " (1 Cor. 15:26). Satan's wiles are still at work (2:11). The age of wickedness is still in force (Gal. 1:4). Even in the church there are enough traces of sin. Hence ceaseless exhortation is necessary, and warnings about judgment.

But the Apostle also affirms: " You are dead, and your life is hidden with Christ in God. When Christ, your life, is revealed, you will also be revealed with him in glory " (Col. 3:3f.). The new creation really exists, but it is still hidden in Christ. Faith is certain of it, and draws its life from it. One day, when Christ himself appears in glory, this new creation will also be manifest in its glory. Till that day comes, the new life is a task which has to be accomplished each day: " As Christ was raised from the dead by the glory of the Father, so too we must live in the newness of life " (Rom. 6:4).

Paul was not a day-dreamer who disregarded or denied the hard facts of reality. And he was not just a prophet whose task it was to point on to salvation in the remote future. He had to proclaim that salvation had already been accomplished, " Now is the hour of grace, now is the day of salvation " (6:2). This was the salvation which had to be laid hold of. Its full perfection still remained to be achieved, but it was really there, certainly and unmistakably. It was Paul's mission to proclaim the two things together: the Now of salvation as well as the Not-Yet of the fulfillment.

In the Book of Revelation, God himself says: " Behold I make all things new " (Rev. 21:5). The renewal of the world in the act of salvation is not just one event which took place in the past, it is something that is always a present happening. God is always active, conquering the past in his forgiveness and his new creation, beginning again and again with man his work of salvation, in spite of man's constant failures. For, " if our heart condemns us, God is greater than our heart " (1 Jn. 3:20).

The Ministry of the Church (5:18—6:2)

¹⁸*But all is from God, who has reconciled us with himself through Christ and has given us the ministry of reconciliation.*

The great event of the new creation cannot be the culmination of natural evolution or the work of man. It can only be the work of God, the creator from the beginning. The deepest truth of the new creation is that now man is given a totally different relationship to God. Sin, which formerly came between them and separated heaven and earth, has been removed. God has taken away sin by creating the state of peace. This work of salvation is a reconciliation.

The concept is taken from the Old Testament. It was one of the main preoccupations and profound needs of the Old Testament to find new prayers and rites by which to reconcile the holiness of God with a sin-laden world and to perform expiation. The law of Moses prescribed the yearly celebration of the great Day of Expiation, with detailed regulation of its ceremonies. When Paul takes up the term and concept of reconciliation, he means that the Old Testament hopes of reconciliation and peace between God and man have now been fulfilled. This was done in the expiatory death of Christ (5 : 21).

The process of expiation is not that an angry God is soothed by the prayers and sacrifices of men. This would be to think of God in a far too human way and one that is unworthy of him. It is God, on the contrary, who acts. It is he who sets up a new relationship between himself and the world, by making the sinner righteous, out of the fullness of his divine righteousness. " He is righteous and makes men righteous " (Rom. 3 : 26). And this again does not mean that God simply forgives because he is always kind and merciful. Forgiveness comes by virtue of Christ's sacrificial death, since he intervened as God and man between God and man and offered the sacrifice of his life in expiation. " When we were enemies of God, we were reconciled with God through the death of his Son " (Rom. 5 : 10). But man is called to accept God's offer of salvation and to allow himself to be reconciled with him.

This God who has accomplished the work of reconciliation and peace has instituted in the church the ministry of reconciliation. The apostles have been charged with the perpetual realization of God's salvific work in the world oppressed by the weight of its sins. The church accomplishes the ministry of reconciliation by proclaiming the grace of God through its preachers and by applying the reconciliation to the faithful in the sacraments (of baptism and penance).

[19]*For God was in Christ and reconciled the world to himself, not holding their sins against them, and instituting among us the word of reconciliation.*

Having said earlier that Christ was the image of God, St. Paul now says that God was in Christ. In Christ, God became manifest to the world. He was revealed as the just and holy God who demanded reparation for sin, which the Son offered on the cross. But God was also revealed as the loving and merciful God who forgave sin for the sake of this expiation, and adopted man as his child through his Son. " Through Christ, God reconciled the universe with himself, all that is in heaven and on earth " (Col. 1:20). " God so loved the world that he gave his only-begotten Son " (Jn. 3:16). " Christ is the expiation of our sins, and not only of ours, but of those of the whole world " (1 Jn. 2:2).

[20]*Thus we are ambassadors who speak for Christ, since God is appealing through us. We ask in the name of Christ: Be reconciled to God.*

The church has been entrusted with the ministry of reconciliation which St. Paul describes in solemn terms. The apostles are ambassadors with a mandate from Christ, taking his place in fact. The word " ambassador " had the same meaning and connotation then as now. The ambassador was the great personage who functioned on behalf of a great king. Christ calls through the words of the Apostle. And since God was and is in Christ, ultimately it is the voice of God which is heard in the voice of the Apostle. The saving hand of God is felt in the ministry of the Apostle. The word of Christ which is thus carried out into the world and the ages is: " Be reconciled to God."

God speaks in the words of the apostles. " You received the divine word of our preaching not as human words, but as it truly is, the word of God which is at work among you who believe " (1 Thess. 2:13). This is certainly true not only of the apostles long ago, but of the apostolic office which lives on in the church, fulfilled today by bishops and priests. We affirm that the preaching of the church is the proclamation of God's word and that in it we hear the word of God. This is in fact the great statement of the New Testament.

[21]*He who committed no sin was made to become sin for our sakes by God, so that in him we could become God's righteousness.*

Once more, in solemn words, St. Paul proclaims the gospel of the salvation of Christ. He explains why the present reconciliation between God and the world is possible, and why we sinners can now be righteous before God. Christ was innocent of sin, but for the sake of others, for us, was turned into " sin," since he bore on the cross the weight of sin. And thus we have been made righteous before God. " Christ has set us free from the curse [on sin] pronounced by the law, since he became for us a curse, as it is written: ' Accursed is he who hangs upon the wood ' " (Deut. 21:23 and Gal. 3:13). A marvelous exchange was made. The sins of men became the sins of the sinless Christ, and his righteousness became the righteousness of sinners. This was possible because one of our race was our brother and also

Son of God. Hence he could take the place of his brothers. And because he was Son of God, his expiation was fully valid before God (Rom. 3 : 22–26).

We do not think that we have fully explained the mystery of the death of Christ when we have expounded it in this way. It is in fact a great mystery that what happened to the one Christ on the cross should have decisive importance for all men before and after this event, decisive for life or death. Nonetheless, Christ himself understood and explained his life and his sacrifice of his life in this way. He said: " The Son of man has not come to be served but to serve, and to give his life for the many " (Mk. 10 : 45). Knowing that his blood was to be poured out for the forgiveness of sins, he instituted, at the Last Supper, the new covenant between God and man (Mt. 26 : 28).

This tells us that none of us is alone. We are all members of a great fellowship and bear its guilt, which we have all added to for our own part. Hence we are lost with this fellowship or we are saved with it. But the message of the gospel is that we are also ordained to salvation by and with that fellowship, of which Christ is the head, who is our brother and our Lord.

[6:1]*Hence we share in the work and exhort you not to have received the grace of God in vain.*

St. Paul concludes his exposition of God's salvific work with a warning. He gives this warning as an apostle who has been called to share in (1 : 24; 3 : 9) the work of reconciliation. God offers the grace of reconciliation, the gift of salvation and peace. No one should receive it in order to waste it. One can indeed receive the grace of God and at least externally accept it. But this can be in vain. God's gift can remain fruitless. Christians are warned to examine themselves to see whether their Christianity is genuine and their conduct fruitful. And if anyone finds himself forced to answer that the grace was wasted, he must make a new start by a new acceptance of the gospel.

²For he says: "At the happy hour I will hear you, and on the day of salvation I will help you" [Is. 49:8]. *See, now is the most happy hour. See, now is the day of salvation.*

The exhortation is supported by a text from the prophet Isaiah. Isaiah speaks of a day still far away from his own times, the day of the coming of the Messiah. St. Paul hears in the saying of the prophet a warning that God gives men an hour of grace which does not come again. *Now* is the hour which the prophet meant. St. Paul stresses it still more strongly. Isaiah speaks of the " happy " hour but for Paul it is the " most happy " hour.

The Poverty and Riches of the Apostolic Office (6:3–10)

St. Paul continues his self-defense. He has always tried to do his work without giving offense. He explains the sacrifices involved in this office in a series of words and clauses which rise in a crescendo, embracing the contradictions and tensions of poverty and riches, of humiliation and glory which are comprised in the apostolic office.

³We give offense to no one in any way, so that the ministry may not be found fault with, ⁴but recommend ourselves in all ways as servants of God, in great patience, in tribulations, in straits and in distress . . .

The Apostle knows that blame which attaches to the person in office often redounds to the discredit of the office itself, whether rightly or wrongly. Hence he dares give no offense.

St. Paul repeatedly refuses to recommend himself in so many words (3:1; 5:12; 10:12). Here he has in mind, however, the self-recommendation which consists of his blameless bearing in the sight of the whole world. Such a commendation is acceptable to him.

We can distinguish three strophes in the following description of struggles, achievements, and sufferings. The first set of phrases are characterized by the repetition of " in " (6:4-7a), and enumerate first a number of situations in which he served and suffered (6:4b.5), and then the charismatic gifts and moral virtues exercised in his office (6:6.7a). Then comes a list, characterized by the word " through," of the circumstances and types of his service (6:7b.8). Finally, there are a number of phrases, each introduced by " as," which describe the basic attitudes of service (6:9f.). In conclusion, the Apostle testifies that he is enabled to bear all this through the inward joy and the riches of spiritual goods which he possesses (6:10).

The apostles are servants of God in a twofold sense: as Christians and as apostles. The disciple is often presented as the faithful servant of God in the parables of Jesus, as for instance in the parable of the workers in the vineyard (Mt. 20:1-16) or the parable of the vigilant serving man (Mt. 24:45-51). Service is the basic and authentic attitude of the disciple, according to the word of the Lord: " He who wishes to be great among you, let him become a servant among you; and he who wishes to be first among you, let him be the slave of all " (Mk. 10:43f.). Furthermore, St. Paul is also servant of God in his character of apostle, calling himself " the servant of the gospel " (Col. 1:23). As an apostle, he is so utterly committed to the service of God

that he is no longer his own master. His primary self-designa-
tion is " servant of God," and this indicates the radical and painful self-renunciation of the apostle who belongs totally to
another, in whose service he labors and toils. From this stem the
various burdens and sufferings which he goes on to enumerate.

First he tells of situations which involve him in suffering.
Patience, according to the basic meaning of the Greek word, is
" holding out under " (suffering). It means steadfastness and
perseverance while waiting for and trusting in the help of God
and eternal salvation. It is indeed a basic attitude of the Christian
life. Tribulations are part of the Christian's existence in the
world. Christians are participating in the passion of Christ, who
suffers in his members (4:10f.). These tribulations characterize
the present time as the last days. Sufferings are, as it were, the
birth pangs of the imminent salvation (Mt. 24:21; Rev. 1:9).

[5] . . . *under blows, in prisons, in tumults, in labors, in sleepless*
nights, in fasting . . .

The Apostle then names some of the hardships which have to
be undergone in the apostolic ministry. They include beatings,
such as the Apostle had to suffer perhaps in mob violence, in the
synagogue, in prison, or before Jewish or heathen judges
(11:24f.). Imprisonment was often the lot of the apostles,
especially Paul himself. The tumults may have been disturbances
and riots in which the Apostle was attacked and his life im-
periled. The labors are the heavy work imposed by his vocation
in all the churches, heavier still in lukewarm disobedient
churches and made still harder again by the resistance of his
opponents. The Apostle had. to experience sleepless nights perhaps in prisons (Acts 16:25), or because his work was so exacting

that he had no time to sleep, or because he also did his apostolic work by night (as at the evening liturgy at Troas according to Acts 20:31), or because the Apostle did manual work by day to gain a living and did his pastoral work at night (see 11:7; 1 Cor. 4:11; 1 Thess. 2:9). The fasting of which he speaks was hardly self-imposed. He is thinking of how he had to go hungry in prison, on his travels, at work, or even simply because he had no money.

⁶ . . . *in purity, in knowledge, in meekness, in kindness, in the Holy Spirit, in unfeigned love,* ⁷ᵃ*in the word of truth, in the might of God.*

Up to this, the Apostle has spoken of being steadfast under trials. Now he speaks of his spiritual gifts and virtues. Purity here does not mean chastity in the strict sense, but innocence and holiness of life in general. Knowledge and insight are manifested by the inspired Apostle as he speaks to the church (1 Cor. 14:6), and it is the task of the Apostle to spread knowledge of the truth (2:14). Meekness and kindness are kindred virtues, which the Apostle has to bring to bear again and again if he is to win men for Christ in spite of all difficulties. That love should be unfeigned is a demand often heard. Only such genuine love can endure. By the " word of truth," St. Paul may mean the frank and sincere way of speaking which he claims is his own. But he may also mean the words of the gospel message, which is the truth and conveys and creates the truth (Eph. 1:13; Col. 1:15; 2 Tim. 2:15). The " might of God " is the power of the gospel at work to save; but it is also the miraculous power bestowed by God on the Apostle (12:12; Rom. 15:19).

[7b]*With the weapons of righteousness right and left . . .*

Now metaphors of warfare are used. The weapons in the soldier's right hand are the sword and spear as offensive weapons, while in his left he carries the shield as a defensive weapon. The Apostle has both types. But he does not use unjust means to fight and defend himself. He uses righteousness. Unrighteousness has its weapons as it fights in the cause of sin (Rom. 6:13), and the flesh has its weapons (2 Cor. 10:4). But the weapons of light are different (Rom. 13:12). Thus the Apostle faces the world as a fully-equipped fighter for righteousness.

[8a]*. . . through honor and contempt, through good repute and ill repute.*

In these verses, 8–10, the language is highly effective, using pairs of words which combine the tension of outward appearance and inner reality and which are linked by their contrasts.

Various opinions are held of the Apostle, and men's verdict on him changes. But such judgments cannot prevent him from going his way and performing his service. Honor and good repute are Paul's lot when dealing with friends and Christians; contempt and ill repute when dealing with enemies. He is despised by Jews and heathens, who bring accusations against him, deride him, beat him, and throw him into prison. He also meets with contempt from his opponents in the church, the pseudo-apostles (11:5), the false brethren (11:26), who slander him and try to hinder his work. And finally, his reputation suffers through Christians who are no credit to him. It is a grave and oppressive burden to meet with dishonor from men (1 Cor. 4:9–11).

[8b]*As deceivers, and still true; as unknown, and still well known,
as dying, and still we live; as chastised, and still not killed* . . .

In the eyes of the world the apostles appear often enough as
deceivers, seducers, and teachers of error. Christians were so
branded by heathens, and by the Jews above all the witnesses to
the Lord Jesus were met with such charges (Mt. 27:63f.). But
the apostles speak the truth according to the verdict of their own
conscience. Their personal conviction here is confirmed by God
and the church. For the apostles are none other than the heralds
who proclaim the truth and reveal it to the world.

They are unknown in the world. Like Christians in general,
they also do not belong to the circles of the " wise, powerful, and
nobly-born " (1 Cor. 1:26). The great world knows nothing of
them, and literature, politics, and science ignore them. They are
not sought after like the famous and imposing personalities of
the time. But still they are well known and appreciated in the
church, and their lives are manifest to God (5:11). Their names
are written in heaven on the eternal tablets (Lk. 10:20; Phil.
4:3). No doubt the apostles are marked by the sufferings and
death of Christ (4:10f.). But from this apparent mortal weakness there breaks out, not indeed human vigor, but the power of
God. Of this the apostles are certain, as they experience the conquest of all sufferings and rescue even from the direst perils
(1:8–10). The chastisements which the Apostle undergoes are
probably his trials and sufferings in general. But they may also
be the chastisements which could be inflicted by law in ancient
times, such as scourging and beating with rods (11:24f.). And
these could sometimes be fatal in their effects. But even when
the apostles are almost clubbed to death, death does not ensue.

St. Paul undoubtedly has Psalm 118 in mind. The psalmist

here regards his tribulations and sufferings as chastisement. " I shall not die but live . . . The Lord has chastised me grievously but he has not delivered me to death " (Ps. 118 : 7f.). So too St. Paul regards his sufferings as a chastisement inflicted by God, who does not cease to love him. " We undergo chastisement, in order that we may not be condemned along with this world " (1 Cor. 11 : 32).

¹⁰ . . . as mourning and yet always joyful, as destitute and yet enriching many, as those who have nothing and yet possess all things.

Distress and tribulation from within and without may well engender mourning. Nonetheless, the oppressed are still full of inviolable joy from their hope in the future salvation. For the " coming kingdom of God is righteousness and peace and joy in the Holy Spirit " (Rom. 14 : 17). From the hardships of prison St. Paul bids Christians on whom the hand of the world lies heavy: " Rejoice in the Lord always. Again I say to you, Rejoice " (Phil. 4 : 4).

The apostles are poor in worldly goods but they have inner riches which they bestow on many others. Their riches are the fullness of their spiritual gifts. " In all things you have become rich in him, in all manner of discourse and of knowledge " (1 Cor. 1 : 15). But their riches are also that of the promised reward. Life has been promised to them. " He who tries to save his life will lose it, but he who loses his life for my sake will gain it " (Mt. 16 : 25). They have heard the assuring words: " Rejoice that day and be glad. See, your reward is great in heaven " (Lk. 6 : 23). The ⁱseer John writes of the church in Smyrna: " I know your tribulation and your poverty. But you

are rich " (Rev. 2:9). From their riches the apostles hand on
consolation and instruction (1:4; 1 Cor. 4:13). They are medi-
ators of God's reconciliation (5:18.20), grace (1:15), and salvation (1:6).

PEACE WITH THE CORINTHIANS RESTORED
(6:11—7:16)

Paul's effort at restoring good relationships and peace between himself and the church at Corinth attains one of its goals in this part of the letter. He rejects once more some unwarranted accusations and asks again for the restoration of fellowship (6:11–13; 7:2–4). The good news brought by Titus from Corinth assures the Apostle in the meantime that confidence has been regained (7:5–16).

Request for Renewal of Fellowship (6:11—7:4)

The two short sections 6:11–13 and 7:2–4 constitute a unity in form and content. St. Paul pleads in ardent terms for fellowship with the church of Corinth. But while making his plea he can already express his assurance that fellowship has been restored (7:2–4).

Cramped or Spacious (6:11–13)

[11]*We have opened our mouth before you, O Corinthians, our heart lies wide open.*

After many rebukes and after his profound teaching on the apostolic ministry St. Paul goes on in the tone of confident dialogue. Here alone we find in the letter the appealing address: " O Corinthians!" He uses what is probably an Old Testament metaphor which means that the heart of one who loves and cares is wide open to welcome all and everything. " You have opened wide my heart " (Ps. 119:32). So too the whole Paul welcomes the whole community. He has spacious room in his heart for the Corinthians. His apostolic office embraces all and leaves no one cramped or oppressed. The breadth of the love in his heart expresses itself in his ardent and impassioned words. The heart and the mouth are mentioned together as in the saying of the Lord, " What the heart is full of, the mouth speaks " (Mt. 12:34).

[12]*You are not cramped in us, but you are cramped in your hearts.*

The metaphor used in the previous sentence is continued. The Corinthians have plenty of room in the heart of the Apostle, but allow him little room. The narrowness of their hearts forbids the Apostle access. What has narrowed and closed their hearts is distrust, suspicion, listening to malicious slanders against him.

[13]*Pay me back in kind—I speak to you as to my children—and throw open your hearts also.*

Paul speaks to his community as a father, in tones of paternal admonition. He begs the Corinthians for a gift in return, that they should be as open-hearted and generous to him as he has been to them. The Apostle is a father to his community. " I admonish you as my beloved children. For though you may have hosts of tutors in Christ, you have not more than one father. For in Christ I have begotten you through the gospel " (1 Cor. 4:14). Through his preaching the Apostle is the father of his community. But the relationship of the Apostle to the church can also be expressed through the metaphor of a mother's love: " My children, for whom I suffer once more the pangs of birth, till Christ is formed in you " (Gal. 4:19f.).

But the church has also preserved the tradition of the saying of the Lord: " Call no one on earth Father; for one only is your Father, he who is in heaven " (Mt. 23:9). The general context of the saying goes on to warn Christians that titles such as " Master," " Teacher," and " Father " should be avoided when speaking of rulers and teachers in the church. Possibly efforts had been made to introduce such titles into the community, perhaps in imitation of the Jewish custom by which the teacher was reverently addressed as " Father." Nonetheless, the title and address of " Father " have become usual in the church, like the title of " Teacher," since a " Doctor " means the same thing. It is hardly thinkable that Paul made Christians address him as " Father." Nonetheless, there is a certain tension between the saying of the Lord and the affirmations in which Paul claims to be father of the community, and indeed also our present-day practice. But no one will appeal to this tension to blame St. Paul or to introduce reforms into our usage. It remains true, however, that the words of the Lord lay down a strict limit. God is so immediately and exclusively close to each man, and in particular to believers, that no man can trespass on this proximity with regard to another and no man may intervene there. The living and life-giving God alone can be truly Father of a man's true life.

Separation from the World (6:14—7:1)

[14]*Do not let yourselves bear a strange yoke along with unbelievers. For what fellowship have righteousness and lawlessness? And what have light and darkness in common?*

The friendly discussion with the Corinthians is interrupted, to be taken up again, however, in 7:2. That 7:2 is the natural sequel to 6:11–13 is all the clearer because in both places St. Paul uses the metaphor of the wide open heart. 6:14 to 7:1 is an interpolation. In form and content it is an admonition, complete in itself, to turn away from the world and to be holy and sinless. The text warns against alliances with unbelievers, and bids Christians choose the proper yoke-fellows. According to 6:16, the unbelievers in question are heathens, not Jews. The Christian life appears as the bearing of a yoke, of which, however, the words of our Lord say: "My yoke is sweet and my burden light" (Mt. 11:30). In 6:14b–16a, five phrases constructed on the same lines make it clear that conformity with unbelievers is impossible. In a stylistic *tour de force*, the notion of fellowship and the coordinates faith and disbelief are designated five times by different terms. The contrast between faith and unbelief appears first as that between righteousness and lawlessness. This is basically the opposition between Judaism and heathenism. The Jew strives hard to keep the law in order to attain righteousness before God. The heathen, who has no (written) law, is a lawless person. Now righteousness has been bestowed on Christians as the free gift of God (Rom. 3:24), and they have to allow this gift to do its work in real life. Thus the ancient contrast between righteousness and lawlessness, which once divided Jews and heathens, now constitutes in a new sense the contrast between the church and the heathen or between faith and unbelief.

Then the contrast becomes that between light and darkness. Terms taken from natural phenomena are used in a transferred sense to speak of the spiritual and moral world. The light is the kingdom of God (Lk. 16:8) and of Christ (Eph. 5:14), while darkness is the kingdom of Satan (Lk. 22:53). The contrast appears again and again in the Gospel of St. John: " The light shines in the darkness, and the darkness did not accept it " (Jn. 1:5; 3:19; 12:35). Hence comes the admonition to those who are called to the light: " You were once darkness, but now you are light in the Lord. Walk as children of the light " (Eph. 5:8; cf. Rom. 13:12; 1 Jn. 2:9).

¹⁵*What accord is there between Christ and Beliar, and what share has the believer with the unbeliever?*

The contrast between faith and unbelief is the same as that between Christ and Beliar, that is, Satan. Christ and Satan often face each other as opponents. In the story of the temptations they appear, as it were, as rival kings, on a mountain high above the world where they fight each other for the world (Mt. 4:8–10). No one can serve these two masters at the same time (Mt. 6:24; cf. Heb. 2:14; 1 Jn. 3:10).

¹⁶ᵃ*What agreement is there between the temple of God and idols?*

The opposition also extends to the region of worship, between the temple of God and idols. The verdict is in line with the faith and institutions of Israel. There the temple of God and idolatrous images formed the ultimate in opposites. The greatest abomination known to the Old Testament was the setting up of idols in the temple. Now the Christian community is the holy temple of God, consecrated by the Holy Spirit. Christ himself compared his church to a lofty house built upon rock (Mt. 16:18). The metaphor is used in various forms by the apostles. The church is, as well as " God's garden," " God's building " (1 Cor. 3:9),

" the temple of God " (1 Cor. 3:16), or " the spiritual house, built of living stones upon the precious foundation stone, Christ " (1 Pet. 2:5).

There can be no agreement between this new, true temple of God and the idols of the heathens. No doubt the heathen religions could acknowledge other gods, just as Rome also admitted foreign gods to its Pantheon, " the temple dedicated to all the gods." But the Christian faith demanded an absolute separation. The council of the apostles obliged Christians to abstain from sacrifices offered to idols (Acts 15:29). St. Paul reminds Christians that since they partake of the table of Christ they cannot also partake of the table of the demons, that they cannot drink of the chalice of the Lord and also of the chalice of the demons (1 Cor. 10:19–22).

In contrast to the gods of the heathens, the Christian God is the living God. The gods of the heathens are dead. In the Old Testament they were called " inanities," " lying gods." The Jews mocked at the fact that the heathen divinities were pieces of wood or lifeless stone. The trunk of the same tree could provide wood to be thrown on a fire, or to be set up and worshiped as a god. St. Paul reminds the Thessalonians that they have turned away from idols to serve the living and true God (1 Thess. 1:9).

He rarely mentions the fact that Christians adore one only God, in contrast to the many gods of heathendom. This is because all his letters are sent to churches which are already firmly established, and conversion from polytheism to monotheism is presupposed as something achieved in the past. Nonetheless, texts like 6:14–16, when taken together with others like Matthew 6:7f.; 1 Corinthians 5:9–13; 8:1–13; 10:7f.; 10:14–22, continue to testify how difficult in reality was the struggle with paganism. Paganism, in the ancient religions or in the refinements and spiritualizations of art and philosophy, still remained a power in the public life of State and society as in the private lives of individuals. Christians were obliged to renounce it completely.

[16b]*For we are the temple of the living God, as God has said: " I will dwell among them and walk among them, and I will be their God and they will be my people "* [Lev. 26:11f.; Ezek. 37:27].

To emphasize and confirm what he has just said in his own words, the Apostle quotes some texts of the Old Testament, which his familiarity with the Bible enables him to interweave. The church is the temple of God. Speaking to the chosen people of the ancient covenant, God had said long ago: " I will dwell among you, and I will walk in the midst of you, and I will be your God and you shall be my people." What was said of Israel under the ancient covenant is equally valid, and indeed more so, of the people of God under the new covenant. It is, as it were, the temple in which God dwells.

[17]*" Depart therefore from the midst of them, and separate yourselves from them, says the Lord, and touch nothing that is unclean. And I will take you to myself "* [Is. 52:11].

Since Christians are God's holy people, they may not defile themselves with heathen abominations. They must leave the world of paganism, though they remain in its midst. They must free themselves and separate themselves from the sins and crimes of unbelievers. The letter uses once more a prophetic text from the Old Testament to inculcate this command. In Isaiah, the text is a summons to Israel to depart from the city of Babylon, which is heathen and therefore unclean. The causes of defilement, according to Paul, are licentiousness, covetousness, and idolatry (Eph. 5:3–5; Col. 3:5). Such impurity is incompatible with the holiness of the church (1 Thess. 4:7). But those who have abandoned the world will find refuge and welcome in God's arms. Christ makes the same promise when he says: "Everyone who leaves his house or brother or sister or mother or father or children or fields for my sake and for the sake of the gospel, will receive them back a hundredfold now in this present time . . . and in the world to come, eternal life " (Mk. 10:28–30).

18"*And I will be your Father, and you shall be my sons and daughters, says the Lord, the ruler of all*" [2 Sam. 7:14].

In its original context, this saying was part of the blessings promised by the prophet Nathan to King David and his son. There God affirms that he will always be a Father to the son of David, the future king of Israel, and that the king can always be confident that he is God's son. The letter applies this divine oracle to Christians in general. God is their loving Father, they are all God's sons and daughters. This is precisely the good tidings brought by Jesus, that God is the Father of his children. The preaching and catechesis of the church hand on these words of Jesus as a precious heritage. Thus St. Paul says that the Christian, under the influence of the spirit of childlike love, is entitled to cry out: " Father, dear Father," and that this is the essential truth of Christian existence (Rom. 8:17; Gal. 4:7).

7:1*Since then we have such promises, dear friends, we must purify ourselves from all stains of flesh and spirit and perfect our sanctification in the fear of God.*

The sayings of the prophets hold good for Christians. But Christians have to recognize the obligations which such promises entail. In particular, the letter insists on the obligation which follows from Isaiah 52:11, as quoted in 6:17. God demands of Christians that they should avoid all stains of flesh and spirit. God has sanctified his elect as he called and chose them, an event made visible in baptism. The sanctification which has been brought about by God in Christians must be perfected by them in moral purity and holiness, with which they must be tirelessly preoccupied.

The letter urges the fear of God upon Christians. But St. Paul also affirms that Christians " have not received the spirit of slavery to inspire them with fear." As sons, they have the spirit of freedom (Rom. 8:15). And we read in 1 John 4:18: " There is no place for fear in love, but perfect love drives out fear." The same word, " fear," has two possible meanings. One is awe for the sacred and majestic; the other is dread of the sinister and evil. The Christian will naturally experience both awe and dread, but he will not be overwhelmed by his anxieties, and he will live in reverent awe, as the Apostle says: " Work out your salvation in fear and trembling. For it is God who is at work in you " (Phil. 2:12f.).

In the Heart of the Apostle (7: 2–4)

²*Make room for us [in your hearts]. We have wronged nobody, we have ruined nobody, we have exploited nobody.*

The statements in 7:2–4 are the sequel to 6:11–13. St. Paul takes up once more his cordial discussion with the Corinthians. He repeats the metaphor of 6:13, asking the Corinthians to make room for him.

When St. Paul denies that he has wronged anybody or ruined or exploited anybody, we may conclude that such charges were being brought against the Apostle by his opponents, more or less publicly. St. Paul has not wronged anyone. Does this disclaimer refer to certain regulations and decisions which he has made, such as the exclusion of an incestuous person from the community (1 Cor. 5:1–13), or to the punishment which he called for in the case of a transgressor (1 Cor. 5:11)? He has ruined nobody. Someone might have been " destroyed " in the above-mentioned cases or in similar ones, either by over-severity or the contrary, by over-indulgence and laxity. Paul, however, is sure that he has not erred. Nor has he taken advantage of anyone's innocence to exploit him. He means, no doubt, financially. Paul earned his living by the work of his own hands and refused to allow the churches to support him. This was to avoid the suspicion of trying to make money by his apostolic office.

³I do not say this to condemn you. For I have already said that you are in our heart, to die together and to live together.

Paul is afraid that he has defended himself so vigorously that his words might sound more like a speech for the prosecution than for the defense. This is a misunderstanding which he wishes to prevent. He is making no accusations and pronouncing no condemnations, and to prove this he appeals to his earlier statements. He had already assured the Corinthians that they were in his heart (6:11–13), that he was pledged to the community for better or for worse, for life or for death (1:6b; 4:12). But the promise of loyalty in death and in life is in fact a not unusual formula, which can be used in various circumstances and can come spontaneously to the lips of the speakers without involving mutual obligations. Thus David's vassal Ithai assures the king: " Wherever my lord the king may be, either in death or in life, there too your servant shall be " (2 Sam. 15:21). But the good shepherd gives his life for those who are entrusted to his care (Jn. 10:11).

⁴I speak to you with great frankness, I speak of you with great pride. I am filled with consolation. I am abundantly rich in joy in all our tribulations.

St. Paul is very confident that unity has been restored between himself and the church of Corinth. He feels he may now speak of everything to the Corinthians with perfect frankness. He knows that they in turn will always understand him correctly. The relationship is one of perfect trust and total open-heartedness. The community is a source of pride for its Apostle. Here he takes up once more and expresses more clearly something which he had alluded to at the beginning of his letter (1:14).

In his letters to the Corinthians, the Apostle is often forced to admit that he thinks of the community with anxiety, pain, and sorrow. Now everything is different. In spite of all his tribulations, he is abundantly rich in joy and consolation. He goes on at once to explain why.

Review of the Dispute (7:5-16)

The statement in 7:5 links up with the story of the Apostle's travels in 2:13. St. Paul now narrates how after a long wait in Macedonia he finally met Titus, who had good news to bring from Corinth. St.

Paul now looks back on the anxious days of his dispute with the church of Corinth. He explains his attitude once more in order to show that his strictness was now justified by its success in bringing the Corinthians to reflect and repent. The easing of the tension is expressed by the Apostle in a language which is almost over-exuberant, in which the words "consolation" (7:6ab. 7ab.13) and "joy" (7:7.13.16) occur repeatedly. St. Paul also uses a number of similar words to describe the changed feelings of the community (7:7.11).

Journey and Report of Titus (7: 5–7)

⁵When we came to Macedonia, our flesh had no rest, but we were beset on all sides with conflicts without and fears within. ⁶But he who consoles the humble, God, consoled us through the arrival of Titus.

St. Paul had reached Macedonia by sea from Troas (2:12f.). He probably stayed at Philippi, the capital of Macedonia, where there was a church very much attached to him. His whole human being and his bodily forces (this is what is meant by "flesh") craved for rest and relaxation. But this was not to be his lot. He was oppressed by conflicts and fears. The conflicts were, no doubt, the attacks made on him by others, which obliged him to defend himself. The fears which beset him were occasioned by his responsibilities for so many churches (11:29), and at that particular time, no doubt, his greatest anxieties were caused by the uncertain situation in Corinth.

The Apostle was rescued from these grave troubles by an overwhelming consolation. His consolation came in the first place from men ("from you," 7:7), but ultimately and most truly consolation comes from God. This is the testimony of good men in all ages: they experience God as consoler, above all the humble, whom God encourages and exalts. " This is my consolation in my misery, that your promise sustains my life " (Ps. 119:50). " The Lord consoles his people and has compassion on his afflicted " (Is. 49:13).

[7]*But not only by his arrival, but also by the consolation with which he had been comforted among you. He told us of your longing, your grief, your zeal on my behalf, so that I rejoiced all the more.*

St. Paul experienced the divine consolation through two events. To meet Titus once more was already consoling. And then Titus had consolation to offer, because he himself had been consoled by the Corinthians. He was able to tell of the longing, the grief, and the zeal of the Corinthians. The longing, being the desire to see Paul again, shows that the Corinthians wished to be in accord and at peace once more with the Apostle and to assure him of their grateful loyalty. The grief of the community attests their regrets for what has happened. They now appreciate repentantly how unjust had been their previous behavior and wish to make reparation. Their zeal shows that they are now ready to acknowledge the justice of the Apostle's claims and wishes, and that they respect his authority in the community which he has served so well. They are ready to make good their past defects.

St. Paul is not ashamed to reveal his human side, very simply and sincerely. He speaks of his depression, his distress, and his anxiety. Human companionship, loyalty, and gratitude console him, and he needs such consolation. In gifts which come to him from men and through men, he experiences and receives the gifts of God. And he gladly counts himself among the humble whom God exalts. He lived in a time when the Stoic ideal was paramount. The sage was to allow himself to be touched by no human emotions and to remain indifferent and tranquil in all circumstances. Paul's notion of man is quite different.

Paul's Earlier Letter
and the Corinthians' Change of Heart (7 : 8–16)

[8]If I grieved you by my letter, I have no regrets. Even if I have regretted it—for I see that my letter troubled you, if only for a while; . . .

St. Paul recalls an earlier letter to the Corinthians and the grief it caused them. This is the letter of which he says (2:4) that he wrote it with great heaviness of heart and with many tears. He finds it difficult now to choose the right words. He is anxious not to say anything hurtful and wishes to avoid further occasions of misunderstanding. He begins by saying that he has no regrets for having grieved the Corinthians. But then he has to admit that he did once regret it. He had no desire, and still has no desire to inflict pain on any church. One of the anxieties which troubled him in Macedonia (7:5) was the fear that his letter might have been inappropriate and have had harmful effects in Corinth. But he no longer regrets the letter now that he sees that the grief of the Corinthians soon passed and brought about repentance. Now he can include the letter in the joy which fills his heart.

[9]. . . now I am glad, not because you have been grieved, but because your grief led to repentance. For you were grieved according to God's will, so that you should not have to suffer at our hands.

St. Paul continues to tread carefully to avoid misunderstandings. Though he repeats once more (as already in 7 : 7) that he is now glad at having written the letter, he adds at once the reassurance that he did not enjoy the discomfiture of the Corinthians, but simply rejoiced at the good effects it produced, since it was responsible for their repentance. The Apostle has, of course, the right to admonish and reprimand, but his conscience would be uneasy if any member of the community was harmed through his fault. Very often the apostolic office imposes difficult decisions on its holders, when they have to choose between various obligations. To take the right decision, they must make every effort to find out what is the will of God.

¹⁰The grief that is according to the will of God brings about repentance without regrets which leads to salvation. But the grief of the world brings about death.

There is a sadness according to God and a sadness according to the world. The former is inspired and measured by God's commandment and will. It brings about contrite repentance which leaves one without regrets. This is a paradoxical situation which St. Paul describes in terms which are deliberately made to seem contradictory. One can never be sorry for true sorrow. A genuine conversion leads to salvation and life, that is, to deliverance at the last judgment. Sorrow according to God brings home to man the truth that the world, as a sinful world, is evil and perishing. He regrets that he has lost himself in such a world. And hence he returns to God by a conversion which leaves the world behind. But the sorrow which is that of a world estranged from God leaves man weaker or makes him obdurate in sin. This sadness of the world oppresses man as he sees that his earthly and fleshly desires are impossible to fulfill. But he remains at their mercy and finally experiences as the world passes away into nothingness the mortal calamity of his own situation.

¹¹Consider then this very thing, that you have been grieved according to God's will, how much good will it has brought about in you, what excuses, what indignation, what fear, what longing, what zeal, what retribution. In every way, you have shown yourselves to be innocent in the matter.

A list of seven good effects shows the blessings of a grief according to God and of repentance. At the same time, St. Paul makes his point once more that his letter was reasonable and justified, though he had to pain the Corinthians by writing it.

St. Paul praises the good will and the zeal with which the community responded to his demands and restored good order. The Corinthians admitted their fault by the very fact that they tried to explain and justify their behavior and asked the Apostle to accept their " excuses." The " indignation " of the community is directed against the guilty parties. The " fear " which the letter occasioned may be fear of the justifiable anger of the Apostle and of the sanctions he might have been expected to impose, but also, no doubt, a general fear of the unhappy consequences which the affair could give rise to. And so the Corinthians were filled with " longing " for the Apostle and with " zeal " on his behalf. A better knowledge and a more just appreciation of the matter also manifested themselves in the readiness to see such punishments being inflicted as seemed right and necessary. Their whole reaction made it clear that the community itself had been innocent in whatever fault it was which called for retribution.

¹²When then I wrote to you, it was not on account of the wrong-

*doer or on account of the person wronged, but so that your zeal
on our behalf should be manifest to yourselves before God.*

St. Paul returns once more to his earlier letter with which he is
so greatly preoccupied, and which has brought so much anxiety
in its wake. He affirms that the only purpose of the letter was to
give the Corinthians the chance to show their zeal and prove
how true it was. It was not to satisfy any personal interests of his
own. St. Paul only hints at what he means, and the actual incident to which he refers is a matter of debate among scholars.
Most probably, he is referring to some offense which had been
given to him personally, an injury of which he had already
spoken (2:5-11). It seems that the community at Corinth did not
call the offender to account at once, but only when they had had
the Apostle's letter (2:4; 7:8).

The point throughout is not that the Apostle wants to be
assured that his rights are upheld, but that the community will
do the right thing. The strictness of the Apostle can also be the
right way of serving the community, when strictness is called for.
Justice must be done. But then there must be real forgiveness.
The community must be brought to repent and amend its ways.
And from beginning to end, the church must act " before God."
It must subsist in the sight of God, for this is life or death. St.
Paul constantly penetrates beyond the immediate and changing
circumstances to what is ultimately decisive, something more
than the legal and ethical aspect, namely God's presence in the
church as he who judges and heals. This insight makes him a
true pastor.

[13]*Hence we are consoled. But in addition to our consolation, we
rejoiced much more at the joy of Titus, because his spirit has
been set at rest by all of you.*

Once more St. Paul recalls with gratitude all that Titus did to restore peace between St. Paul and the community. Titus had gone to Corinth as St. Paul's messenger, with anxiety and trepidation. But he found good will among the Corinthians and experienced the warmth of their friendship and zeal. This relieved his mind and gave him joy and consolation. If St. Paul was already consoled by hearing that all was in order at Corinth, he now had an additional cause of joy when he saw the happiness of Titus. The human and brotherly affection of St. Paul is shown by the fact that the joy of others is also a joy to him.

[14]If I said anything to him in praise of you, I was not made ashamed of my words, but just as we have spoken the truth in all we said to you, so too our praise of you to Titus has been proved true.

Before sending Titus to Corinth to restore peace between himself and the community, St. Paul had spoken of his pride in the community as a whole, in spite of whatever faults it had. It is characteristic of the kindness of St. Paul as a man and a pastor that he always finds something good to say of others. He was not put to shame before his fellow workers. The Corinthians justified his praise of them, and the words of St. Paul were proved true. He goes on to make his assertion still stronger: in everything that he had said, he had spoken the truth, and his truthfulness is proved. It follows that he had been reproached with being unreliable, and St. Paul found the charge of insincerity very hurtful. He comes back to it again and again (1:17f.; 4:2).

[15]And his heart goes out to you all the more as he thinks of the

obedience of you all, how you received him with fear and trepi-
dation. [16]*I am happy that I can rely on you in all things.*

Titus has been extraordinarily well received in Corinth. He was
not merely relieved and overjoyed by the attitude of the Corinthians, but his heart went out to them, in a movement of affection which was constantly renewed and deepened when he
thought of the welcome which he had been given at Corinth.
St. Paul undoubtedly thinks of the relationship between apostle
and church in terms of warm affection, and this is his actual
attitude to the community. But he does not lose sight of the
office and its authority, which are equally real in this relationship. The community owes the apostle its obedience, and indeed,
it is only proper that they should receive him with fear and
trepidation. This fear is not human dread of the superior power
of another man. Titus had no such power with regard to the
Corinthians. And such fear would be incompatible with the
virtue of freedom (1 : 17). But St. Paul is speaking of the
reverence and obedience due to his office, through which God
works in the church (5 : 19f.).

Finally, St. Paul assures the Corinthians of his unalloyed joy
at seeing peace restored. He knows that he can have complete
confidence in them.

THE COLLECTION FOR THE CHURCH OF JERUSALEM (8:1—9:15)

The theme which runs through chapters 8 and 9 is the commendation and organization of the collection to be made in Corinth for the church in Palestine. These two chapters form a very distinct unit in the letter. On one of his visits to Jerusalem, St. Paul had pledged himself, when speaking to the apostles and the churches there, to make such collections in his churches (Gal. 2:10). He had already spoken of the matter in his first letter to the Corinthians (1 Cor. 16:1–4), and a year or so after sending the second letter he was able to give news of the completion of the collection (Rom. 15:25–28). 2 Corinthians 8 and 9 link up with 7. Now that the fullest confidence reigns once more between St. Paul and the Corinthians, he can lay this request before them. 8:7 takes up and follows from 7:7.11, even verbally. In other respects chapters 8 and 9 are also linked with the preceding, in as much as they continue to describe the experiences, plans and activities of St. Paul (1:15f.; 2:12f.; 7:5–7).

The Good Example of the Churches in Macedonia (8:1–5)

Before asking the Corinthians to make a collection for the church in Jerusalem, St. Paul announces that the collection in Macedonia had been highly successful. He is writing this from Macedonia, and hence the happy experience is still fresh in his memory.

The letters of St. Paul and the Acts of the Apostles show only too clearly how much hostility he had to experience from the Jews in Jerusalem, and even from Jews there who had become Christians. He was persecuted by the Jews for teaching that the gentiles were now the object of God's election, after Israel's rejection of its Messiah.

And narrow-minded Jewish Christians reproached him for refusing to recognize that the ritual law of the Old Testament still obliged the church (Acts 21:21). His adversaries pursued him into his missionary territories. He was often forced to protect and stand up for the churches which he had founded in the freedom of the gospel, against adversaries who tried to denigrate him personally and impose on all Christians the observance of the Jewish law of the Old Testament as an extra burden. The adversaries against whom St. Paul had to defend himself in Corinth were also associated with this Judaistic agitation. Nonetheless, St. Paul refuses to forget, and will not allow the Christians converted from paganism to forget, that the gospel started from Jerusalem in its march across the world, and hence that all peoples owed a heavy debt of gratitude to the primitive community in Jerusalem. Hence the churches composed of gentile Christians, St. Paul infers, are debtors with regard to the mother church of Jerusalem. It was from there that they received the spiritual gifts of the gospel and it is only right and proper that they should return thanks with earthly gifts (Rom. 15:27). " Salvation is from the Jews " (Jn. 4:22) is a truth which holds good for the church in the time of St. Paul, for the church and the Christian world in general, and even for a completely secularized world.

8:1We now tell you of the grace of God, brethren, which was given to the churches of Macedonia . . .

The collection made in Macedonia is also mentioned by St. Paul in his letter to the Romans: " Macedonia and Achaia have decided to make a collection for the poor among the saints in Jerusalem " (Rom. 15:26). From the letters of St. Paul and the Acts of the Apostles we know of three churches in Macedonia at Thessalonica, Beroea, and Philippi (Acts 16:11—17:14). Corinth was the capital of the province of Achaia, and the funds raised by the collections were pooled here.

The collections were a manifestation of the love which was

powerfully at work in the community. But this love was not an achievement of their own virtues, but a grace of God bestowed upon them. It is always a grace, when men are ready and able to give and help. For the natural thing is that men should earn money primarily for themselves and enjoy it only themselves. The thought of the grace of God is particularly dear to St. Paul, and the term recurs again and again in chapters 8 and 9. The church's work of love is the fruit of the grace of God which is active in it (8 : 4.6.7.19). The church received this grace and favor in Christ (8 : 9), and this gift of grace is bestowed on all and is immensely rich (9 : 8.14).

². . . so that in spite of being tried by many tribulations, the superabundance of their joy and their abysmal poverty gave abundantly, in the riches of their simplicity.

This heavily-loaded sentence describes the charitable work of the Macedonians. The greatness of their love may be seen from the two contrasting elements which entered in. The churches were being sorely tried. Nonetheless they responded with profound joy, a joy which flowed over into gifts. And then, they were and are in great poverty in outward things. Hence the lavishness of their gifts was not due to the fact that they were rich. Nonetheless, the inner riches of their simple kindness became manifest thereby. Thus it can be seen that in their faith and life the churches display the same contrasts of poverty and riches as the Apostle himself.

³As well as they were able; I swear, and beyond what they were able to do, of their own free will ⁴they begged of us the favor of being allowed to share in this service on behalf of the saints.

The Christians of Macedonia acted spontaneously, impelled by a free resolve which was wholly their own. The gifts of the churches were not merely according to their means, but well beyond their means. They had not to be urged to give, but considered it a privilege and favor to be allowed to give, and hence came forward themselves with the request to be permitted to share in the common undertaking of helping the saints (see 1 : 1). Otherwise they would have felt obliged to regard themselves as excluded from the fellowship of the church.

⁵And not only did they do that, as we had hoped, but they gave their own selves, to the Lord in the first place, and then to us, according to the will of God.

The success of the collection surpassed all expectations. When they gave of their possessions, something much more profound took place. The Christians gave their very selves. They threw themselves into the work personally, indeed, they sacrificed themselves, to help others. The sacrifice was made, primarily no doubt, for the sake of the needy, but ultimately it was a dedication of self to the Lord and his apostles. The Macedonians understood that what was at stake was not just the relief of the poor in certain churches, but the cause of the gospel and of the Lord of the church and God himself. In serving the church, Christians ultimately seek and serve Christ and God, just as the service of God must always take the concrete form of serving the brethren.

But the Macedonians also sacrificed themselves for the Apostle. For they knew how much St. Paul had at heart the collection for Jerusalem. As his servant, St. Paul may place himself beside his Lord (as 4:5). This is the order of things which has been instituted by divine law in the church. But all took place according to the will of God. It was through the grace of God that this self-sacrificing love came into play.

The Collection in Corinth (8:6—9:15)

St. Paul explains and justifies the taking of a collection in Corinth as well by a number of motives. He mentions the zeal of the churches in Macedonia (8:8). He desires that the church of Corinth should be rich in this grace as in so many others (8:7.10f.). He recalls Christ as the model of self-sacrifice (8:9). And finally he mentions a motive which could be a natural one appealing to right reason—though he at once supports it by an appeal to scripture—that equality should be brought about between superabundance and want (8:14f.).

Exhortation (8: 6–15)

⁶*Therefore we asked Titus to see that this work of love was completed among you, just as he had already begun it.*

Encouraged by the great success of the collection in Macedonia, St. Paul had asked Titus to bring to completion the work (which St. Paul terms once more a grace of God) which he had already begun at Corinth. Hence, at an earlier visit to Corinth, Titus had started to organize a collection, or had put new life into a collection which had been started by order of St. Paul (cf. 1 Cor. 16:1).

Possibly Titus had set his hand to the work during the visit just mentioned (7:5-15), during which—after restoring peace between St. Paul and the Corinthians—he might also have been able to take over the matter of the collection. But now Titus is with St. Paul, at the time of the writing of the present letter, our

" second," to the Corinthians. Titus is to go back to Corinth, from which he has just arrived, and bring the letter with him. During his new stay there he is to bring to completion the work of collecting alms for Jerusalem.

[7]But just as you are superabundantly rich in all things, in faith and speech and knowledge and great zeal, and in the love which flows over from us to you, so too you must be superabundantly rich in this grace.

The church of Corinth is richly endowed with graces. It must also be rich in the grace of works of charity. Among the graces of the church, the first mentioned are faith and speech and knowledge. Faith is not an achievement but a gift. The word and the notion of faith are very full of meaning. Faith is undoubtedly knowledge and mastery of the doctrines of faith, but it is also and above all the believer's attitude as an expression of confidence and dedication. The " speech " of which St. Paul speaks is the word of revelation which is spoken to the church, which is received by the church, which each one is bound to confess for the instruction and conviction of others, and which has been bestowed on the Corinthians in many forms as inspired doctrine. Knowledge, finally, is the understanding of faith and true divine wisdom, for which all must strive and which will be given to all.

The gifts of zeal and love are given special prominence by their place at the end of the list. They are also signaled by additional characteristics and more specifically defined. The love is that which has been enkindled by St. Paul, cherished by the Corinthians, and given back in turn to the Apostle. Zeal and love are the special marks of the relationship between the

Apostle and the church of Corinth. Now they are to bear fruit
in works of charity.

*⁸I do not mean this as an order, but I should like to test the
genuineness of your love against the zeal of others.*

St. Paul wishes to avoid giving the impression of any sort of
unwelcome compulsion. He does not wish to " constrain " the
church in any way (cf. 1 Cor. 7:35). Above all in the matter
of the collection he is unwilling to give direct orders. Nonetheless, he speaks and acts with his apostolic authority. By remind-
ing his readers of the zeal of the churches in Macedonia, he
seeks to test and prove the sincerity of the love of the Corinthians, since love is the touchstone of faith and of knowledge
(1 Jn. 3:17f.). The Apostle is entitled to test the Corinthians in
this way, but only the Apostle. The love in question is the love
of the Corinthians for the poor communities in Palestine, but
also their love for St. Paul, who is so keenly interested in the
collection, and finally also the love which unites them to God,
on which all other love is founded. The all-embracing character
of the word love is revealed at once in the sequel.

*⁹For you know the grace of our Lord Jesus Christ: being rich,
he became poor for your sakes, so that through his poverty you
might become rich.*

In the middle of his considerations about the relationships
between the churches, St. Paul points to the example of Christ,
thereby suddenly revealing the theological depths which underlie
very realistic and earthly things. Christ renounced the divine
fullness of power in which he dwelt with the Father, abandoned

the heavenly glory which was his as the Son of God. He chose
the poverty of human existence so that through his poverty he
could impart the eternal riches of redemption to the poverty of
all for whose sake he became poor. In the same way, other
apostolic exhortations, bidding Christians to think not of their
own but of others' good and welfare, point to Christ, who for
the sake of man emptied himself of the divine riches at the
incarnation (Rom. 15:3–7; Heb. 12:2). The hymn to Christ in
the Epistle to the Philippians likewise calls for self-sacrifice in
the light of Christ's example (Phil. 2:5–11), and expounds in
detail the doctrine here presupposed—that of the nature of
Christ, and his way from divine eternity through earthly time
and back to eternity. This is the grace which Christ has given
to the world. But if his poverty made the Corinthians and all
men rich, those who have been so abundantly showered with
gifts should now in turn give to others with sincere love. The
action of Christ must continue in the life of Christians.

The grace which should impel the Corinthians to the charitable work of the collection is threefold. It is the grace bestowed
on the Macedonian churches (8:1). It is also the grace which
should be powerfully at work in the Corinthian church (8:6f.).
And finally, it is the prototype of grace which has become visible
in Christ (8:9). In all three cases St. Paul employs the same
word "grace." The meaning common throughout is: self-
dedication brought about by the gift of God.

*¹⁰And here is my opinion on the matter. For the work will be of
benefit to you, since you have begun a year ago not merely to act,
but to cherish the desire.*

Once more St. Paul affirms that he is not giving a command
but only encouragement. The work of charity will also bring

benefit to the Corinthians. He is thinking of the tangible benefit which each good deed also bestows on the doer, by strengthening moral attitudes and resources. And the Christian will grow in faith and love. The work of collection in Corinth had already been going on for a considerable time. The Corinthians had launched the effort in the previous year. The idea and the plan, and above all the execution, had been their own initiative. It is enough to remind them of this. It will not be necessary for the Apostle to issue commands.

¹¹But now go on and complete the work, so that, just as you were willing to undertake it, you also complete it, in accordance with your means. ¹²When the willingness is there, it is acceptable in accordance with the means it has, not in the light of what it has not.

Since the Corinthians decided long ago to take up a collection, they must now carry out their resolution in full. To give assurances of one's willingness means nothing. What counts is the deed in the end. But giving must be in accordance with one's means. St. Paul makes another effort (cf. 8:8) to ensure what he always has at heart, that the Corinthians should not feel the collection to be an imposition. He asks them to do nothing unreasonable or exaggerated. They are to make a contribution in keeping with their resources. For good will and sacrifice are judged acceptable, not by the quantity given, but by its relation to one's resources. St. Paul does not ask for the impossible and no one is asked to give what he has not got. But even a small gift can be a testimony of love and a real sacrifice. We are reminded of the gospel story of the widow's mite (Mk. 12:43f.). St. Paul's restraint in urging the collection is justified, because the majority of the faithful in Corinth and certainly in the rest of Achaia (according to the indication given in 1 Cor. 1:26), were poor.

[13]*It is not to be a relief to others and a burden on you, but a matter of equality,* [14]*so that at the present time your abundance may help those who are in want, and their abundance supply your needs, so that there may be equality . . .*

It is not intended that the gifts should aid the recipients, while the givers put such a strain on their resources that they themselves should be reduced to distress. All that is aimed at is an equality in the goods necessary to sustain life. The Apostle's attitude is very balanced and his words very sober. When speaking of the churches in Macedonia he does not hesitate to say that in spite of their great poverty, they gave not only according to their means, but beyond their means (8:3). His own rule of life in his apostolic ministry is to sacrifice himself for others (12:15). His dying is the life of the community (4:12). But no one can or ought to be urged or compelled to do the extraordinary.

Equality between the needy community in Jerusalem and the other Christian churches is to be brought about in two ways. In the immediate present, the abundance of the other churches should be used to help the distressed community of Jerusalem. But aid will flow back from Jerusalem and its abundance will then also supply the needs of the other communities. How and when is this to happen? Does St. Paul mean that the church of Jerusalem will repay the gifts in kind? Does he think it possible that one day the communities of Jerusalem will be affluent and the others reduced to poverty? But surely he means some-

thing different? In the letter to the Romans he also calls for a
collection for the poor of Jerusalem. And he explains it by saying
that the gentile Christian communities had shared in the spiritual
good things of Jerusalem and hence owe the church in Jerusalem
a debt, which they must repay by helping with " fleshly," that is,
material goods (Rom. 15:27). Must we therefore conclude that
in our present text St. Paul is assuring the Corinthians that
Jerusalem will still continue in the future to enrich the gentile
Christians from its superabundance of spiritual gifts? Or does
his assurance mean that the support given to the church of
Jerusalem will be richly repaid to the givers through the thanksgiving which will be offered to God for their generosity?

15. . . . *as the scripture says: " He who had much had no superfluity, and he who had little was not left short "* [Ex. 16:18].

To conclude, St. Paul supports his exhortation by appealing to
an example from the Old Testament. He affirms that what
happened at the miracle of the manna will take place once more.
Some of the Israelites gathered more, others less, but in the end
each of them found the same amount in his vessel, but all had as
much as they needed. What took place miraculously in the
desert is to be repeated in the Christian churches by the exchange
inspired by brotherly love.

Mission Sent to Corinth (8:16–24)

16*Thanks be to God, for he filled the heart of Titus with the
same good will towards you.* 17*Titus agreed to my request.
Indeed, his good will was so great that he [offered to] set out
to come to you of his own accord.*

St. Paul's intention is to send Titus to Corinth with other companions, to take up the tasks which await them there. They will
have a new recommendation from St. Paul when they present
themselves there. Titus gladly accepted the charge, and St. Paul
is so glad to find Titus willing and eager that he cannot be
content simply to state the fact, but must speak of it with heart-
felt gratitude towards God. His thanksgiving means that he sees
Titus' readiness as a gift from God.

Titus has the same zealous care for the church in Corinth as
St. Paul himself had. Indeed, he was far more eager than his
obligations towards the Apostle might have demanded, so that
his journey to Corinth, from which he had just returned (according to 7:6), is undertaken not in consequence of the Apostle's
command but of his own free will.

[18]*But we send with him the brother whose praise in the cause
of the gospel resounds throughout all the churches.*

St. Paul attaches to Titus two companions (8:18.22) who are to
support Titus and also St. Paul himself in the taking of the
collection. Each of Titus' companions is presented separately and
in a different way. They obviously have different ranks and tasks
in the service of the churches.

St. Paul does not give the names of the two companions
assigned to Titus. The fathers of the church found this surpris-
ing, just as exegetes of the present day also ask themselves who
they may have been and why their names are not given. Their
names cannot be divined. Possibly they are Christians whose
names crop up elsewhere in the New Testament, possibly their
names are not mentioned at all. St. Paul could easily have
omitted their names in the letter if the people in question were

not known to the Corinthians and if he was leaving it to Titus to introduce them by name to the Corinthian church.

St. Paul says of the first of the companions of Titus that his praise in the cause of the gospel resounds throughout all the churches. He was therefore a preacher or church leader of high standing and universally known. The " cause of the gospel " can mean either the actual preaching of the gospel or include also services rendered to the church.

[19]*And furthermore, he was chosen by the churches to be our traveling companion in this work of grace, which is carried on by us for the glory of the Lord and in which we show our own good will.*

On account of his high reputation everywhere, this companion assigned to Titus had already been appointed by the churches to work side by side with St. Paul in making the collection for Jerusalem. This piece of information gives us a glimpse of the government of the church in the earliest days. When St. Paul appoints this representative of the churches, who already has certain official duties to perform, and is also his own traveling companion and helper, to go with Titus, he is not acting entirely on his own initiative. The churches have the right to make their own choice, which they do by taking a general vote. Once more, St. Paul speaks of the collection which is being made, not as a human achievement but as a grace of God. But the grace of God makes itself felt through the service performed by men. The end and object of the collection of alms is the glory of God, though it also serves the purpose of demonstrating the eagerness of the Apostle to serve the church in every way. In particular, this work of charity is to make known to all that St. Paul acknowledges the special place of the primitive church of Jerusalem, that he wishes to remain linked to it, and that he continues to urge the whole church not to forget its obligations to Jerusalem as the mother church.

²⁰But we are anxious that no one should speak ill of us, in this matter of the rich gift of which we have the charge.

If St. Paul has been assigned helpers and companions in the work of the collection, this is a measure which is entirely in accord with St. Paul's own wishes. He is happy to be able to forestall all suspicions. He is hardly afraid of the crude accusation of applying some of the money fraudulently to his own use. But he might be suspected of using his authority as an apostle to exploit the communities, his ultimate aim being still his own advantage, if he thought to use the alms to win for himself the friendship of the recipients. St. Paul had already had to defend himself against such charges (1 Thess. 2:5), and according to the present letter (12:16–18), though he accepted no support from the church in Corinth, his adversaries still accused him of exploiting the church by means of his delegate Titus and other envoys. Hence he had good reason to be on his guard against hostility.

²¹For our purposes are honorable, not only in the sight of the Lord but also of men [Prov. 3:4].

St. Paul confirms the principle on which he acts by quoting a saying from the Book of Proverbs (as in Rom. 12:17). He is concerned about his good reputation in the eyes of men. He knows, of course, that he and his fellows are held in disrepute by the world (1 Cor. 4:10), and that he has to carry out his ministry through honor and dishonor, in good repute and in ill repute (2 Cor. 6:8). The seemingly contradictory statements must be explained by the fact that the Apostle tries to avoid giving any unnecessary offense, so that no one will be scandalized where the scandal is not intrinsic to the Apostle's mission. But he is also aware that his person and his preaching must give such scandal often enough and that he must take the consequences. It is the Apostle's task to reveal the truth, and his sincerity before God should therefore be made apparent to all men of good will.

²²We are also sending with them our brother, whose true zeal we have often experienced, but who is now even more zealous, being fully confident of you.

The second companion whom St. Paul sends along with Titus is presented differently from the first. He is St. Paul's brother, that is, brother in Christ or perhaps also brother in office of St. Paul and Titus. But nothing else is said of his previous service to the church. Hence he probably had not yet served the churches in an independent and public capacity, though St. Paul had personally known him as a zealous helper on many occasions and esteemed him accordingly. His eagerness to go to Corinth and serve the church there surpasses all his previous achievements.

²³Whether I am commending Titus—he is my companion and fellow worker among you; or our brothers—they are apostles of the churches, the glory of Christ.

St. Paul sums up his exhortations in brief statements which are also striking appeals. He characterizes once more the three helpers who are to go to Corinth to supervise the collection. He honors Titus by affirming that he has been his familiar companion at all times, but above all, his fellow worker when dealing with and serving the church of Corinth. The Christians sent along with Titus have their dignity from their relationship to the church and to Christ. They are apostles of the churches. Here, as in many other places, St. Paul uses the title " apostle " not merely of the twelve apostles who were called by Christ himself, but of a wider circle of office holders in the church. " Apostle " means " envoy," an envoy of the gospel or an envoy used by the churches to communicate with one another. St. Paul says that they manifest the glory of Christ to the world. When speaking of ecclesiastical office in general (3:8–11), he affirms that it is the revelation of the radiant majesty of God. Hence he can also say of the individuals who hold office in the church that they manifest to mankind the power of Christ's redemption and his grace.

24So, in sight of all the churches, give proof of your love and justify our praise of you to them.

The Christians of Corinth are now to prove that their love of the brothers is genuine by demonstrating this love in the concrete instance of the church of Jerusalem. But they must also demonstrate that the praises which St. Paul had heaped on them, as he boasted of them to the messengers before they set out, were justified and accurate. The Corinthians are to do this by welcoming his envoys open-heartedly and by supporting them with their help, but above all by being generous with their gifts. The church of Corinth is to remember throughout that everything takes place in public, under the eyes of the whole church.

Visit of Paul in the Near Future (9:1–5)

9:1I need write no more about the service to be done to the saints.

Just as 8 : 23f. summed up and rounded off a section, so too 9 : 1 is a fresh start. Nonetheless, chapter nine, repeating chapter eight to some extent, continues to treat of the matter of the collection. The whole of chapter 8 was devoted to the collection and so is chapter 9. If then in 9 : 1 he still says that he need write no more about the service of the saints (as embodied in the almsgiving), he can only mean that he has nothing further to say about technical details, its organization and execution. And in fact he does not dwell further on such matters. According to 1 Corinthians 16 : 1–4, he had already made certain arrangements. He may have made further arrangements in person, at a visit to Corinth, if such a visit, the so-called " intermediate visit," had taken place between the first and second letter to the Corinthians. Finally, these matters may have been left also to Titus and his companions to arrange, since it was precisely in view of the collection that they were going to Corinth.

²I know of your willingness, of which I speak with pride to the Macedonians when speaking on your behalf, saying that Achaia has been ready since last year; and your zeal has stimulated many.

St. Paul also, no doubt, considers it unnecessary to write in detail, because the essentials are assured beyond question, that is, the eagerness of the community at Corinth. He has told the Macedonians, with whom he is staying at the moment, that Achaia, the province of which Corinth was the capital, has been ready for a year. The news was a powerful stimulus to the Macedonians. This was true at least of the majority of them. Hence there were still some who did not take part.

³I am sending the brother, so that our boasting of you may not prove vain in this regard, so that you will be ready, as I affirmed, . . .

One of the reasons why St. Paul was glad to have helpers along with him in the work of the collection was to avert the suspicion that he was himself hoping to benefit by it (8:20). He now gives further reasons for sending the workers in advance. He had boasted of the zeal of the Corinthians when speaking to the Macedonians. Now the advance party was to prepare and launch the collection. St. Paul reminds the Corinthians of how painful it would be to him if his words of praise should be proved to be baseless. He adds politely, " in this regard." The other points on which he had spoken in praise of the Corinthians would not be affected.

4. . . so that, when the Macedonians come with me and do not find you ready, we—not to mention you—may not be made to rue this confidence.

St. Paul has particular anxieties when he contemplates his further travel plans. He intends to go to Corinth in the near future, along with some Christians from Macedonia. He would not like to have to feel ashamed of the Corinthians before the Macedonians. But he corrects his statement by adding that it would be the Corinthians themselves, and not Paul, who would be put to shame.

5Hence I thought it necessary to ask the brothers to go to you before me, and arrange in advance for your blessed gift to be ready, as promised, so that it may really be a blessing and not an exaction.

Inspired by such oppressive emotions and fears, St. Paul considered it necessary to urge the brothers to go ahead of him and see that the collection was in order and as abundant as he hoped. He now designates the collection by a new term, " blessed gift." It is a gift which comes from the grace of God and from God's blessing on the givers (8:1; 9:8). And it should be a gift along with which the givers wish to bestow happiness, blessing, and salvation on the recipients. Hence the gift must be a generous one and must testify that it was given joyfully, and not just begrudgingly under compulsion.

The Blessing Brought down on the Giver by the Gift (9:6-15)

⁶For it is true: He who sows sparingly will reap sparingly and he who sows a fullness of blessing will also reap a fullness of blessing.

The exhortation to provide alms for Jerusalem is followed by a section, 9:6-15, which in part contains general exhortations to works of charity, for which it gives motives, and in part gives further reasons for supporting the collection for Jerusalem. Two thoughts in particular come to the fore. Generosity will not impoverish. For God rewards the willing giver with good things and blessings (9:6-10). Then, the gratitude of the recipients will find its most profound expression in thanksgiving to God as the giver of all good things. Hence charitable works lead to the end and object of all history, that God should be glorified by all the world (9:11-15).

The section, especially in the first part, is interwoven with Old Testament quotations or allusions. St. Paul follows the spirituality of the Old Testament and shares its confidence. Almsgiving was considered as a divine command in Israel and was liberally practised. And Israel was certain that God's blessings were showered on the pious and charitable.

The possibilities of liberal or sparing gifts of which 9:5 had spoken are discussed further. They are like seed sown by men, and the harvest will correspond to the sowing, according to God's recompense. The harvest is used as a metaphor to describe the recompense allotted in God's judgment. We find it in the Old Testament, when the prophet speaks of the judgment on the nations: " Put in the sickle, for the harvest is ripe!" (Joel 3:13). It is also found in the New Testament, where the last judgment is compared to a harvest (Mt. 13:39).

7Let each one give as he has resolved in his heart, feeling neither sad nor under compulsion. For " God loves the cheerful giver " [Prov. 22:8].

St. Paul appeals for generosity in giving. It must not be from a sense of compulsion. Quoting the proverbial wisdom of Israel, he says that God loves the cheerful giver. Gifts must be distributed not reluctantly and disconsolately, but with a happy eagerness. " If you are helping the needy, do so with cheerfulness " (Rom. 12:8).

8God is powerful, and can give you every gift in superabundance, so that in all things and at all times you may have a full sufficiency and still have a superfluity for all good works, 9as scripture says: " He has distributed largesse, he has given to the poor. His righteousness abides for ever " [Ps. 112:9].

The gracious gifts by which God distributes reward are very lavish. They do not merely restore what was given, and not

merely bestow on the giver all he is in need of, they also supply
a superabundance, so that he can do new works of charity. God
rewards generosity by constantly giving new means of making
gifts. Experience teaches that generosity does not impoverish.

The exhortation is confirmed by Psalm 112, which depicts the
ideal of the upright man. The good man scatters largesse to the
poor in all directions. And his righteousness abides for ever.
In the original text, the psalm affirmed that the memory of the
just will be cherished for ever. The original sense of the text
may also have been in St. Paul's mind. But perhaps he also
means (according to 9:8) that God will fill the just man with
such an abundance of good things that he will always be able
to exercise his liberality; or perhaps again, that God rewards the
righteousness of the good with eternal recompense.

¹⁰*But he who gives seed to the sower and bread for food will
also bestow seed on you and multiply it. May he also make the
fruits of your righteousness abound.*

Alluding to the words of the prophet (Is. 55:10), St. Paul recalls
that it is God who in his provident kindness furnishes the
sower with seed and man with the bread which grows from the
seed. God will also show himself to the Corinthians as the God
who gives such gifts. He will provide them with seed, that is,
what they contribute to the collection for the primitive community. But he will multiply the bread that grows from it, that
is, give all that they are in need of for themselves. St. Paul then
prays that God may also bestow on them abundant fruits of
righteousness, quoting the prophet Hosea (Hos. 10:12). God, he
hopes, will grant that the charitable works of the Corinthians,
one of which is the collection for Jerusalem, may continue to

expand. Their love and their kindness will increase, and the resources they have at their disposition will only grow greater, the more generously they give.

[11]In all things you will grow rich in great generosity, which through us brings about thanksgiving to God.

The riches with which God rewards the benefactor are, according to 9:8.10, the abundance of earthly and spiritual gifts which enables him to be even more generous. Another consideration is now added. Just like the giver, the recipient recognizes the gift as God's blessing. Hence the benefaction makes the recipient burst into thanksgiving to God. The giver causes God to be acknowledged and praised by his creatures.

[12]The service of this liturgy [i.e. sacrificial gift] will not only provide for the needs of the saints; it will also show its superabundance through the many thanksgivings which will be offered to God.

The charitable work which is planned has a twofold aim and effect. First it will provide for the needs of the church of Jerusalem. But above and beyond this, it will be transformed into a rich blessing. For the gifts received will cause many prayers of thanks to be offered to God as the gracious giver of all love. St. Paul here actually uses the word " liturgy " to speak of the collection which is planned. The word meant originally " work done in the service of the public " and can have a secular or a religious sense. The latter is probably also envisaged here, and hence the collection is a consecrated sacrificial gift for the fellowship of the church. Thanksgiving and

praise offered to God by the church, and through the church
the acknowledgement of God in creation, is the final end to
which St. Paul constantly refers events (1:11; 4:15). The liturgical worship of God is in his eyes one of the essential tasks
of the church. It lives by the riches of the gifts which it receives
from God, and its thanks go up to God in return. In all that
the church does the glory of God is the beginning and the end.

¹³*On account of the well-proved quality of this service, they
praise God for the obedience of your confession of the gospel of
Christ and for the pure generosity of your fellowship with them
and with all.*

St. Paul is speaking of the reception of the gifts by the church
of Jerusalem and of the effects which they will have there. The
Jewish Christians there will find that the Christianity of the
community of Corinth, and hence of the gentile Christians, is
well-proved, tested, and true when they receive a generous gift.
When they see this work of charity, they will recognize that the
pagans too have become obedient to the gospel of Christ. They
will recognize that all are one, in one single attitude and fellowship, ready to help and full of love. For all this, the mother
church in Jerusalem will not only be grateful to the generous
benefactors behind the collection, they will also thank and praise
God for his glorious work in the church.

¹⁴*And in their prayer for you they long for you on account of
the superabundant riches of God's grace towards you.*

To the praise of God who has called the gentiles to the faith, the
church of Jerusalem will also add its petitions for the church

of the gentiles. It will long to proclaim, in one way or another, the fellowship which it shares with them, among whom God's grace has brought about such generous kindness. Once more (cf. 8:1.6f.; 9:8.10) St. Paul says that the work of charity in the community is not its own achievement but the gift of God to them.

We know from the letters of St. Paul, as well as from the Acts of the Apostles, how anxious he was that peace reign between himself, the church of the gentiles, and the mother church in Jerusalem which consisted of Jewish Christians. The collection was also meant to serve this purpose. This is only hinted at in the second letter to the Corinthians, but not long afterwards, in the letter to the Romans (15:26–32), St. Paul speaks of it openly. The collections for Jerusalem taken up in the gentile Christian churches are intended to maintain peace and unity in the church. But there he also confesses that he has great misgivings as to whether the collections will be well received in Jerusalem and have the happy effects hoped for (Rom. 15:32). The confident hopes which St. Paul expresses in our present letter were hardly fulfilled. He brought the collection personally to Jerusalem at Pentecost in the year 58 (Acts 21:15–26). But even the attitude of the Jewish Christians in Jerusalem was not friendly, while the Jews pursued Paul with mortal hatred. They plotted to assassinate him, and it was only the Romans who saved him, when the governor of the occupied territory took him into protective custody (Acts 21:27—24:27).

15Thanks be to God for his gift beyond praise!

The collection at Corinth has not yet been brought to completion. It still causes St. Paul great anxieties. He knows that the matter will still demand much effort. But his confidence in the power and grace working in the church is greater than all his doubts and anxieties. Hence he finally voices his conviction that the result of the collection will be a considerable sum, that the love of the community will superabound (9:12), and that the grace of God will be immense in all (9:14). But this is only part of the incalculably great gifts of God's grace. Inspired by this certainty of faith and hope, he concludes with thanksgiving for the work of God's grace. This is his final perspective—the ultimate source of all good, even of that which comes through men. But God's grace, immeasurably full and unfathomably deep, cannot be grasped or described, and is beyond human utterance.

A Final Consideration

These two chapters provide apostolic commentary and directives on institutions like collections, dues, and organized works of charity which were and remain necessary in the church. But even when speaking of such earthly things as money, St. Paul remains truly " before God in Christ " (2:17; 12:19).

The Apostle himself had to learn by hard experience how much effort the organization of such things demands. The collection which had been planned and launched a year earlier in Corinth was making only slow progress (8:10; 9:2), so that St. Paul found it almost a painful subject (9:3–5). In spite of all urging, some refused to participate (9:2). The Apostle appoints helpers, whom he asks to promote the collection and bring it to a conclusion (8:6.16–24). As always (7:12; 1 Cor. 5:4), the Apostle cannot and will not simply give orders, especially in such matters (8:8.10). There is to be no compulsion (9:7). St. Paul has to take pains to try to convince the people involved, and ultimately it is the force of his own love which must flow over into the church and stir it to action (8:7). The demands must not be ill-considered, but must be tempered in view of what is practical (8:11f.). The administration must be such that all false suspicions are averted (8:21). The money collected is the property of the church, and hence in these matters above all the community has the right to be brought into the discussion and to be given its share of responsibility (8:16–21). These principles are models of sobriety, and should ensure a careful and conscientious administration of church property.

All these matters seem to be worldly necessities which have invaded the church. But even here it is true to its nature, which is to be a divine institution in the world. Almsgiving and works of charity were already a law binding the people of God of the Old Testament (8:15; 9:7.9.10). The works of love are a realization of the priestly service of the church (9:1.12f.). The authenticity of the universal fellowship is made manifest in the mutual care of Christians for each other (8:4). A gift of money is a sacrificial gift (9:12). It is a way of testing and proving true the love which unites the fellowship (8:8; 9:13). This love spontaneously seeks to join in the almsgiving (8:3). The universal bond grows stronger and stronger through the love with which the recipients respond to the givers (9:14). When the faithful are poor in worldly goods and in distress themselves, the spiritual riches of the church are disclosed in their gifts (8:2). These riches consist of faith, speech, and knowledge as well as love (8:7). To give beyond one's means is a great grace (8:3). When making financial and material sacrifices, the believer dedicates himself to the Apostle as servant of God, and to the Lord of the church himself (8:5).

The helpful love of the church must give effect to the example and love of its Lord, who emptied himself in order to help the poor (8:9). Hence works of charity are a test of the church's obedience to the gospel (9:13). In such activity, the church manifests the power which works within it, the gift of God and the life of God. By virtue of this service, all men can see the grace (8:1.6f. 19; 9:8) and the blessing (9:5) which the church has received. Only those who have received the grace of God can lend their aid. If they can give, it is only because God had first made them rich (8:1.6). But the giver will be granted riches and superabundance in view of good works (9:8–11). All works of charity are produced and blessed by God.

The ultimate goal of all help given by Christian to Christian, by church to church, is that thanks be returned to God for his grace, and that the grace given to the church be acknowledged and praised before the world (8:19; 9:11–13). Loving service becomes and remains service of God. " Let your light shine before men, so that they see your good works and praise your Father who is in heaven " (Mt. 5:16).

SETTLING ACCOUNTS WITH OPPONENTS IN CORINTH (10:1—12:13)

Chapters 10—12 are generally considered to form a section to themselves in 2 Corinthians. In style and content they are a self-contained unity, being a very personal apologia and an indictment in which St. Paul makes a devastating onslaught on his opponents and tears to shreds the criticisms which they have leveled against himself and his work. They are a revelation of the forceful personality of the Apostle as he gives vent to his anger, condemns the guilty, and imposes punishment. But behind it all is the sincere and ardent love of the father and pastor who is only intent on serving the church for which he cares so intensely.

Paul on Himself (10:1–11)

In the first section of the great apologia, St. Paul defends himself by examining and refuting a number of accusations made against him by his opponents. One of these accusations may be deduced from 10:1a. It is that St. Paul, when he is away from Corinth, is very courageous and vigorous, but that when he is actually facing the Corinthians, he is very humble. Another of the accusations must have been, according to 10:2b, that the Apostle is inconsistent and hesitant "according to the flesh." A further accusation, according to 10:10, was that his letters were powerful and imposing, but that his personal appearance was insignificant and that his spoken word was unimpressive. St. Paul refutes the spiteful charges, though he admits that he walks "in the flesh," that is, that he is no more than human. He affirms, however, that in the struggle which he carries on he is not "fleshly" or a prey to human weakness. He is field-marshal in a mighty campaign to win the whole world for Christ (10:3–6).

Paul's Conduct (10 : 1–2)

[10:1]*Now I, Paul, appeal to you, by the gentleness and sweetness of Christ, I who am humble when among you, but at a distance very bold.*

The name " Paul," emphatically prefixed, indicates the beginning of the new section. The Apostle is deeply and personally committed in what follows. His words are given special weight by his holding up the model of Christ to the Corinthians. He appeals by virtue of the gentleness and sweetness of Christ. Christ himself had spoken of his own gentleness: " Take my yoke upon you, and learn from me, for I am gentle and humble of heart " (Mt. 11 : 29). Possibly St. Paul wished to remind his hearers of such sayings of Jesus. But more probably, he is urging them to think of the humble life which Christ led on earth, going around doing good to all, undergoing unresistingly violence and contumely in his passion, and finally giving his life for others. Christ was the humble servant of all, as he himself affirmed: " The Son of man has not come to be served but to serve " (Mk. 10 : 45). This is how the church also saw the life and passion of Jesus: he did not defend himself and uttered no threats, but committed his cause to the just judgment of God (cf. 1 Pet. 2 : 21–23).

St. Paul recalls the gentleness and sweetness of Christ, because he was reproached with being bold at a distance, though no doubt he was humble and yielding when face to face with the Corinthians. He was said, therefore, to be without the very virtues which the example of Christ's life demanded. His retort is that he is perfectly well aware of the example which he is obliged to follow. But in saying this, he is also urging the

Corinthians to strive after the same virtues. For he had had
to rebuke them for the disobedience and quarrelsomeness which
had harmed and even threatened to destroy the good relations
between themselves and the Apostle. The Corinthians too were
in need of the gentleness and sweetness of Christ.

This verse is important for the personality of the Apostle Paul.
In his personal contacts, as the accusation runs, he is yielding
and even feeble and cowardly. But at a distance he is energetic
and violent, just as his letters when he is away use strong words.
St. Paul mentions this charge several times, which means that he
did not treat it lightly. Was the accusation completely baseless
or was there some sort of occasion for it? He says of his first
appearance at Corinth: " I came before you weak and full of
fear, in much trepidation " (1 Cor. 2 : 3). Certain indications in
2 Corinthians have led some scholars to suppose that before this
letter was written, Paul paid a visit to Corinth, in the course
of which he failed to make any headway against his opponents
(2 : 5; 13 : 2). He also affirms that he does not intend to experience distress once more at Corinth (2 : 1). Hence he was afraid
that there might be more clashes. When writing of his activities
in Thessalonica he says: " Though as apostles we might have
been exigent, yet we were as gentle among you as a mother
nursing her children " (1 Thess. 2 : 7). Was there therefore
something about St. Paul which enabled the malevolent to say
that he was personally feeble and unimpressive? His opponents
at Corinth cannot imagine that the restraint he imposes on himself is due to his love and his care for his Christians. They
interpret everything in a hostile and spiteful way, and their
harsh criticism finds ready hearers.

2I only ask that when I come I need not display such boldness as

*I think I could bring confidently to bear on some who think that
we walk according to the flesh.*

St. Paul makes no attempt to explain and defend his previous
behavior. But he assures his readers that he will demonstrate his
resolution against the people who reproach him with walking
" according to the flesh." Here " flesh " does not mean sinful-
ness, or inclination to sin, as would be the strict meaning of the
word, but a way of life determined by personal interests and
earthly considerations. These are not St. Paul's motives, such
things as human respect, cowardice, vanity, covetousness, pride,
or arrogance. The discussion which follows takes up such
questions.

Paul's Weapons in His Fight (10:3–6)

³*Though we walk in the flesh, we do not fight our battles
according to the flesh.*

St. Paul accepts the charge of his opponents, that he lives in the
flesh, but not that he lives according to the flesh. He admits that
his life is a human, bodily one, but not that he behaves and
fights according to the flesh, that is, inspired by selfish desires.
Having already described the service of the missionary as that
of a soldier of Christ (6:7), he now goes on to develop the
metaphor.

⁴*The weapons of our struggle are not fleshly, but divinely powerful to destroy ramparts, since we can destroy [false] arguments . . .*

The apostles may be compared to the generals in a mighty campaign, the objective of which is to win the whole world for Christ. The weapons used, as St. Paul describes them, are not fleshly, which would mean that they were ultimately impotent, but overwhelmingly powerful. The terms and metaphors are taken from the Old Testament, where it is often said that Israel's weapons of war are not weak and earthly like those of its enemies, but strong with divine force. In this march of the gospel, mighty ramparts are taken and pulled down—the citadels of seeming human wisdom and sophistry. St. Paul is perhaps thinking of such texts as: " The wise man captures fortified cities and destroys the ramparts on which the godless rely " (Prov. 21 : 22).

⁵. . . *and everything high and mighty which challenges the knowledge of God, and capture all minds for the obedience due to Christ* . . .

In the spiritual war there are lofty citadels to be stormed, the pride and haughtiness which rear their heads against the true wisdom of God as it advances irresistibly to triumph on earth. Once the citadel is stormed, the garrison is taken prisoner. The minds which try to resist the knowledge of God, of Christ, and of the gospel are won over and brought under obedience towards Christ. Intellect and reason are not to be eliminated but used, though in the obedience which St. Paul calls " the obedience of faith " (Rom. 1 : 5). Hence the use of compulsion is excluded in this " war." Faith can never be forced on anyone by external coercion. The unbeliever must be won over for the faith by the work and words of the apostle, and ultimately by the call and the election of God's love. Once captured by faith, thought attains to the wisdom of the perfect (1 Cor. 2 : 6f.).

⁶. . . and are ready to punish all disobedience, once your obedience is complete.

Even the punishment of the disobedient does not take place by means of earthly force. This was not at Paul's disposal. The punishment is inflicted by means of the spiritual authority by which the Apostle convicts disbelief, puts it to shame, and banishes it from the world. St. Paul is determined to conquer all disbelief on earth. But first the church of Corinth must be perfectly united and obedient in faith. Only then will the Apostle be able to undertake other missionary work.

These words were written when the church in the world, and in the eyes of the world, was nothing but a small religious sect of which there were many in the religious and spiritual movements of the time. St. Paul is well aware that the apostles are utterly unknown to men (6:9). But here we have a vision of a world mission which testifies magnificently to the lofty consciousness of the Apostle and the faith of the church. The whole world is the field of the gospel, and the world is one day to be united in faith!

Paul's Authority (10:7-8)

⁷Look at what is before your eyes. If anyone is convinced that he belongs to Christ, let him in turn consider this: that just as he belongs to Christ, so do we.

St. Paul appeals to common sense, asking the Corinthians to look at the obvious facts. Then he takes up something that may have been used as a slogan. Many claim to " belong to Christ " and deny this of St. Paul. How is this possible? There were four parties in Corinth, who called themselves after Paul, Apollo, Cephas, and Christ, each maintaining that they belonged in a special way to their patrons (1 Cor. 1:12). It seems that we now hear the same claim to belong to Christ as was put forward in these disputes by the party in question. Possibly these opponents appeal to Christ alone, possibly even to special revelations from Christ, and refuse obedience to St. Paul and perhaps to the church itself. They play off their pretended " special relationship " to Christ against the church. St. Paul shows how impossible are such claims. He too belongs to Christ. Any partisan claim to fellowship with Christ which excludes others is impossible. Have disunited and quarrelsome Christians always remembered this?

[8]If I were to boast still more about the authority which the Lord has given me, for your edification and not for your destruction, I should not be put to shame.

St. Paul has expressed himself almost too modestly. He could have been somewhat more emphatic in his boasts, without having to fear that he could not make good his claims. For he is not just a Christian, but an apostle called directly by Christ. Hence he can truly affirm, like his opponents, that he belongs to Christ. As an apostle, he has the authority and the mandate to build up the church. He said in 10:4 that he had the charge of tearing down, but now it is to build up. The contradictory statements are easy to understand, and both are true. The apostolic office must tear down what is false and build up what is true and abiding in the faith. The prophets had the same twofold service to accomplish, as Jeremiah said : " See, I set you today

over peoples and kingdoms, to destroy and to pluck up, to build
and to plant " (Jer. 1 : 10).

When St. Paul says that he has the right to boast, he uses a
word and takes up a subject to which he must come back again
and again in the sequel. His opponents, the false apostles, boast
of their office and of their achievements. St. Paul denies them
the right to do so, but is reluctant to counter their self-praise by
boasting in turn. It is only after a long struggle with himself
that he comes to boast, and when he does so it is for the sake
of his office and not for his personal aggrandizement. Even then
he does not boast of his achievements, but only of the revelations
granted to him, of his sufferings, and finally, of his weakness
(12 : 1–10).

Quite apart from the present occasion, one of the decisive
questions of human existence and self-understanding, in the
eyes of St. Paul, is whether man may boast at all. Man tends to
be proud in the sight of God of his accomplishments and virtues.
He refuses to admit that he is a sinner and in need of the grace
of God. Hence his boasts are an expression of man's self-assertion, pride and unbelief (see 1 : 12).

Paul's Letters (10 : 9–11)

⁹*But I do not wish to seem to try to intimidate you by my letters.*
¹⁰*His letters, they say, are weighty and forceful, but when he
comes in person he is feeble and as a speaker he is worthless.*

Having rejected complaints about his person and his ministry,
St. Paul takes up the criticism of his letters which was already
touched on (10 : 1), and deals with it at length. He is not afraid

of the accusation of trying to intimidate only by written messages which break down on closer examination.

His opponents say that his letters are weighty and forceful, possibly on account of the lofty consciousness of his office and the self-assurance which St. Paul displays there as he reprimands, punishes, and demands obedience. But possibly they may be thinking of how much he demands of Christians. In any case, they say, his personality is unimpressive, his appearance is insignificant, and as a speaker he is poor. When compared with other missionaries, perhaps they found him lacking in the artistic diction and the impressive eloquence, such as Apollo for instance could call upon, " an eloquent speaker, well-versed in the scriptures " (Acts 18:24). Apollo worked with St. Paul at Corinth, and hence many adhered to him and cut themselves off from St. Paul (1 Cor. 1:12; 3:5). St. Paul himself says of his preaching: " My words and my preaching were not the persuasive words of wisdom, but gave proof of the Spirit and power " (1 Cor. 2:4). He even admits that he is a " bungler in his speech " (2 Cor. 11:6). It seems that some, or perhaps many at Corinth, and undoubtedly his opponents, were very sensitive to such defects in St. Paul, and hence failed to sense and experience his spiritual force. This would be characteristic of a community formed in the culture of the Greeks, such as Corinth. The Greeks treasured eloquent and witty discourse above all else.

[11]*Such people should bear it in mind that when we come, we shall show ourselves the very same in action as we have appeared in our letters while absent.*

St. Paul can only reaffirm that he is well able to show himself no different when present than when absent, that his actions will correspond to his letters. This is probably a hint that he will take action when he next comes if forced to do so. At the end of the letter (13:1f.) he actually promises to take action.

Paul and His Opponents (10:12–18)

Having refuted the objections of his opponents, St. Paul now makes grave charges against these men. He accuses them of being interlopers in his missionary territory, of trying to take over from him the churches he has founded and displace the founder. They have no sense of discretion, moderation, and good order, and merely disturb the church. To counteract their line of conduct, St. Paul points to his own sure consciousness of having been charged by God to carry out his ministry, a task which he may not renounce. His duty gives him his rights, and his rightful position imposes on him a duty. He passionately defends both his rights and his duty (10:13–15). Here his language, especially in the Greek, is awkward and complicated. Some sentences seem to have been left unfinished. This betrays his excitement, but often makes the translation and interpretation of the text uncertain.

The Unbridled Boasts of the Opponents (10:12)

¹²We do not presume to compare ourselves or to equate ourselves with certain persons who recommend themselves. But since they measure themselves against themselves and compare themselves to themselves, they are senseless.

This is obviously ironic. St. Paul says he does not dare to compare himself with his opponents, meaning of course the opposite. They think that they are great men, because they recommend themselves, and are foolish enough to take themselves as the standard of comparison when measuring greatness. They lose sight of reality in their pride.

The Measure of the Apostle (10 : 13–16)

¹³*But we refuse to make unmeasured boasts, and keep to the measure of the rule which God has allotted to us as a measure, namely that we were enabled to come as far as you.*

In contrast to the foolishness of his opponents, St. Paul knows that he is boasting in accordance with the task and the grace which God has allotted to him. St. Paul was enabled to reach Corinth and found the church there. Such an achievement is in fact beyond man. The Church is always God's foundation and work. Hence the existence of the church at Corinth is proof that God has been working through St. Paul. His claim to be the true apostle of Corinth is confirmed by God. The Apostle was the measure allotted to the Corinthians, just as they were the measure he was to use. Hence St. Paul has the right to boast of the church of Corinth.

¹⁴*We are not over-extending ourselves, as though we had not really reached you. For we actually reached as far as you with the gospel of Christ.*

Since St. Paul was the missionary who came to Corinth, he had not trespassed beyond the limit set him by God. He was the first messenger of the gospel to appear at Corinth. The opponents came later, and so are branded as interlopers.

*[15]We do not boast beyond all measure on the basis of others'
work, but we hope, as your faith grows, to grow great among
you, according to the measure we use, and reach the greatest
heights . . .*

St. Paul, when he boasts, is not staking his claim on land where
others have done the work. But he has to reproach his opponents
with trespassing on the field of his labors. They are appropriating
the work of others when they put themselves forward as apostles
of Corinth. Their boast is false. Having spoken of his previous
missionary territory, the Apostle now hints at future missionary
activities and travel plans. For the moment the church at Corinth
needs his ministry. It must first be given a full and firm foundation in faith. According to the task and measure allotted him by
God, St. Paul desires to grow to the fullest possible height, by
completing this work.

*[16]. . . in order to preach the gospel beyond your boundaries, but
not in another's allotment, to boast of what is already accomplished there.*

Once this base is assured, St. Paul hopes to go on to preach the
gospel in lands beyond Corinth. But he does not intend to pene-
trate the territory allotted to others, or lay claim to work already
done and boast of it.

What he means is made clearer in the letter to the Romans,
which was composed at Corinth. Here too he begins by saying:
" I have made it a point of honor not to preach where Christ
was already known, so as not to build on others' land " (Rom.
15:20). He goes on to say that he has preached the gospel in a
great circle from Jerusalem to Illyria. He has no more room in

these territories and intends to pay a short visit to Rome, and then to travel on to Spain.

True Pride (*10 : 17–18*)

¹⁷" *He who wishes to boast, let him boast in the Lord* " [Jer. 9:22f.].

St. Paul recalls a saying of the prophet Jeremiah which seems to him to confirm his own considerations. When the prophet says: " He who wishes to boast, let him boast in the Lord," he means, when his words are applied to what has just been said, that all must be done according to the rule and measure established by God the Lord. It is this God who has also called the missionaries and allotted them their spheres. St. Paul's conscience is clear, since he knows he followed this rule.

¹⁸*For it is not the man who recommends himself who is qualified, but he whom the Lord recommends.*

St. Paul's opponents disregarded the divine order of things. To appeal to one's own recommendation and praise proves nothing. Praise is valid only when given by others, as the proverb says: self-praise is no praise. But St. Paul goes on to say that even praise from other men can never be ultimately decisive. Only the man whom God the Lord has tested and recommends has been validly judged and definitely approved of. How does this come about? In the office to which the Lord calls his servant; through the gifts which he gives him; through the blessings with which he crowns and confirms the work of his servant. This principle was also accepted by Christ: " If I give testimony to myself, my testimony is not true. There is another who gives testimony to me " (Jn. 5 : 31f.).

To all hostility and reproaches, St. Paul opposes his assurance of being called by the Lord to his service, and of being approved and recommended by him. This concludes the first part of the debate.

Paul's Boast on His Own Behalf (11:1–12:13)

Having established against the foolish self-praise of his opponents that only boasting in the Lord is permissible and meaningful (10 : 18), St. Paul now seems, in chapter 11, to imitate his opponents and so commit the folly of self-praise which he has just denounced. For he affirms that he is convinced of the folly of his undertaking (11 : 17), which he begins by professing openly. He starts again and again to praise himself, but only to break off each time (10 : 7f.13; 11 : 5.16.19 21.23.30; 12 : 1.11), finding the foolishness too much for him. For it is not according to the Lord, but according to the flesh. It is a shameful undertaking (11 : 21a). But after stubborn resistance, he recounts, as though carried away by passion, all the human and earthly privileges, as well as the heavenly and divine ones, which he can claim (11 : 21b—12 : 10).

St. Paul adopts the bearing of his opponents. He behaves like a braggart trying to bring down his rivals, partly by self-praise and partly by denigration. But from behind the mask of self-praise, he utters nothing but the full truth, which is therefore all the more convincing for the open-minded and all the more shattering for his opponents.

Paul's Request for Patience with His Boasting (11:1–3)

¹¹:¹*I should like you to bear with a little folly from me. But please bear with me.*

St. Paul expresses a wish to the Corinthians, knowing already
that it is granted. It may be surmised that he is being ironic,
though the object of his anger is not yet clear. He asks the Corinthians to put up with a little of his " folly." The word may have
been a slogan of his opponents, who made some such charges
against him (5 : 13; 11 : 6f.21.23). We only learn later what the
folly is—the role of braggart which St. Paul will now adopt
(cf. 11 : 16).

²*I am jealous for you with God's jealousy. I betrothed you to
one man, to lead you to Christ as a pure virgin.*

To start with, St. Paul does not speak at all as a fool but very
seriously. The Corinthians will be patient, as he has requested,
because they know how devoted he is to them. He is impelled
only by his loving care for the church of Corinth.

His relationship to it is described in a metaphor. The church
is the bride of Christ and Christ is the bridegroom. The Apostle
is the father of the bride who escorts her to her bridegroom.
In this capacity St. Paul watches jealously over Corinth. Having
helped to bring about the espousals and joyfully assented to
them, the father watches carefully over the bride to protect her
from harm and keep her true to her promise. As father of the
church (6 : 13), this is St. Paul's attitude towards Corinth.

His jealousy is good, because it is such as God has and it
stems from God. God was passionately interested in Israel's
holiness and fidelity, jealous of the Baals, the gods who tried
to seduce Israel into apostasy from its God. He uttered the
threat: " You shall not worship the false gods. For I, the Lord
your God, am a jealous God, who visits the sin of the fathers
on the children of those who hate me, unto the third and fourth

generation " (Deut. 5:9). St. Paul has the same feeling of jealousy about the purity, sincerity, and fidelity of the church of Corinth. His second letter to this church is a vivid expression of this wooing.

St. Paul's zeal, however, is not on his own behalf. It is all on behalf of Christ, to whom he has espoused the bride. It is for Christ that she must remain intact in her undivided loyalty. The purity of the bride would be endangered not so much by moral seduction as by false doctrine and erroneous convictions about the faith (11:4). Purity of doctrine is of supreme importance to St. Paul. Like St. Paul, the church has preserved it jealously in all ages.

The purpose of the espousals is to lead the bride to the bridegroom. In the marriage customs of which St. Paul was thinking, this took place when the bride was escorted from her father's house to that of her bridegroom, presented to him, and accepted by him. In other words, it was in fact the marriage. In the figurative usage of St. Paul, the marriage is the return of Christ at the end of time. When he comes in glory, the bridegroom Christ must find the church of Corinth awaiting him loyally. It will have to appear before Christ to be judged by him. If it is found holy, it will be united with the Lord. The same care obtrudes itself again and again on the Apostle—to warn the church to have itself immaculate for the day of the coming of Christ (1 Cor. 1:8; Phil. 1:10; 1 Thess. 5:23). For the return of Christ is not seen by St. Paul and the church of his day as an event which is reserved for a very distant day in the future. The church lives for this day, which can take place at any time. Hence its whole life is dominated by a sense of responsibility towards a Lord who is very near. This gives the church the proper attitude to all things: " Brothers, the time is short.

Therefore, those who have wives must be as though they had them not; those who weep, as though they wept not; those who rejoice, as though they rejoiced not; those who buy, as though they possessed nothing; those who use the world, as though they had no dealings with it. For the reality of this world is passing away " (1 Cor. 7 : 29–31).

[3]But I am afraid that just as the serpent deceived Eve in his cunning, so too your minds may be perverted from a single-minded devotion towards Christ.

As the father watches over his daughter against seducers, so too St. Paul over the church of Corinth. The words which the Apostle uses are charged with reminiscence of the story told in Genesis 3, of the seduction of Eve by the serpent. He is afraid that just as Eve was misled by listening to its cunning talk, instead of being simply obedient, so too the church of Corinth could be deceived by a seducer and forget its undivided loyalty to its bridegroom.

It would be corrupted if it did not abide by the pure gospel as St. Paul had delivered it, but adopted the doctrines of the intruders.

THE CHURCH AS THE BRIDE OF CHRIST

We are familiar with this metaphor, which is frequent in doctrine and spirituality today. The present text of 2 Corinthians is its first clear use in the New Testament. It has its roots in the Old Testament. The prophet Hosea, who lived in the eighth century B.C., used the image of married love to describe the

relationship between God and Israel. The God of Israel addresses his people as follows: " When Israel was young, I took
it to my heart " (Hos. 11:1), and, " I betroth you to me for
ever, I betroth you to me in justice and righteousness, in steadfast love and compassion, I betroth you to me in faithfulness,
so that you know the Lord " (Hos. 2:19f.). Israel was often
unfaithful, but God's love did not cease. Israel consoled itself
with this pledge of God's love. Hence the metaphor of the
marriage between God and Israel was used again and again in
later writings (cf. Is. 54:4-8). The time when the Messiah was
to come to his people was envisaged as a marriage festival
celebrating the union of God and his people. Jesus in turn
described himself as the Messiah-Bridegroom of the community
of his disciples. When they were reproached with not observing
the strict fasts of the pious, Jesus defended them by saying:
" Can the marriage guests fast, as long as the bridegroom is
with them? As long as they have the bridegroom with them,
they cannot fast " (Mk. 2:19). Here Christ himself indicates
that he is the bridegroom of his community, and that it is a
festive time, since he is with it.

St. Paul took up the comparison and used it frequently.
According to Romans 7:3f., Christ and the church are united
as though in marriage. According to Ephesians 5:22-32, the
mysterious union of love between Christ and the church is like
a marriage, and union is the model for every earthly marriage.
The image is also used in the visions of Revelation, where the
end of time brings the marriage feast of the Lamb with the
church, gloriously adorned like a bride (Rev. 14:4; 21:2.10;
22:17). The image used elsewhere in the New Testament of the
church as a whole is applied here by St. Paul to a simple community. The whole church is represented in each local church.

Paul and the " Super-Apostles" (11 : 4–6)

⁴*If anyone comes and preaches another Jesus whom we have not preached, or if you are offered another Spirit whom you have not received [from us] or another gospel, you accept it willingly.*

Before coming to his promised folly, St. Paul allows himself a digression (11 : 4–15) in which he characterizes the opponents who threaten to corrupt the church of Corinth and hence force him to speak like a fool. In the severest terms, he finally pillories his opponents as pseudo-apostles and ministers of Satan (11 : 13–15).

There is great danger of the community's being seduced like Eve. St. Paul knows how readily the Corinthians welcome other teachers and other doctrines. What teachers and doctrines has he in mind? He says that the strangers bring with them a three-fold gift which is fraught with danger: another Jesus, another Spirit, and another gospel. The opponents combated by St. Paul in 2 Corinthians not only attacked him personally but also tried to introduce strange doctrines. They had already met with some success, at least insofar as the community was giving these teachers free rein, and so playing with fire.

The terse allusions of St. Paul makes it difficult to say what these false doctrines were. But this at least seems probable: they were proclaiming " another Jesus." St. Paul says again and again in this very letter to the Corinthians that Christ entered life through his death, and that his disciples must also enter life through death. Were these teachers trying to take an easier way, preaching that one could have share in life without dying daily? And was this why they were proud of their achievements, regarding them as works entirely produced by themselves

(10 : 13.17)? They have " another spirit." The Apostle is full
of the Spirit of God, as is his preaching (1 Cor. 2 : 4; 7 : 40;
1 Thess. 1 : 5). " Another preaching " must come from " another
spirit," but not the true one. And they have " another gospel."
The one gospel which St. Paul knows, and which excludes all
others, is the preaching of righteousness which God bestows on
faith without the works of the law. He saw the unbelief of Israel
in the fact that they sought to merit righteousness through their
works. And St. Paul's opponents in Corinth point proudly to
their Jewish ancestry (11 : 22). This means, no doubt, that they
called on Christians to continue to perform the works of the
Old Testament law if they wished to be righteous before God.
But St. Paul teaches that Christ has set us free from the law
(Gal. 3 : 13). If the law has still to be fulfilled, Christ has died
in vain (Gal. 2 : 21).

⁵But I think that I am in no way inferior to these super-apostles.

St. Paul calls his opponents " super-apostles." They act as if
they were superior to everyone, and possibly even think they are.
Hence the ironic title. No doubt they claim the title of " apostle "
and are given it. However, this title in St. Paul is not confined
to the twelve, the first apostles, but is given to the messengers
of the gospel in general (8 : 23). Hence they could be super-
apostles in the widest sense.

In his denunciation of the false apostles, St. Paul goes on to
say that he may be unschooled in rhetoric, but not in knowledge
(in Gnosis, 11 : 6). St. Paul's letters are as forcible in condemning
a false Wisdom, that is, a false Gnosis, as a false Judaism. This
Gnosis was a religious and philosophical movement which had
then spread very widely in the world of antiquity. It held that

there were two godheads, a good one and an evil one. The evil godhead had created the world, which was therefore evil and to be abstained from as far as possible. Gnosis further taught that there were many intermediate beings between God and the world and considered Christ as one of such beings. St. Paul saw that such a doctrine would destroy the gospel, which taught that the heavenly Father was the creator of the world, and that the world was the object of his care and was good. Gnosis also destroyed the gospel which taught that Christ was the Son of God, the one saviour of mankind. The opponents of St. Paul were no doubt influenced by this Gnostic movement or attracted by it, or were at least playing with it. The Apostle fights resolutely for purity of doctrine.

⁶I may be a bungler at speaking, but not in knowledge, for in every way we have revealed it to you in all things when address-ing you.

St. Paul's opponents maintain that in all important matters he is their inferior, which also clearly included the accusation that he was unschooled in rhetoric. This he admits, saying that he is a bungler when it comes to speaking. He was educated at Jerusa-lem in the schools of rabbinical learning (Acts 22:3), of which his letters give proof enough in their interpretation of the Old Testament, which is true to the tradition of the schools. Hence the accusation can only mean a lack of training in Greek rhetoric, in which, however, a cultured man of his day was expected to be formed. This deficiency in St. Paul was remarked on at Corinth, the city of Greek philosophy and art, as is indi-cated also by 1 Corinthians 1:17. When conceding his weakness here, St. Paul denies that it is anything essentially important. His lack of eloquence is compensated for by the depths of his knowledge. This knowledge, science, and wisdom was not learned by St. Paul in any school. It is the science of the gospel, given him by the Spirit of God. The " mystery of God, hidden since eternal times " was revealed to him (Rom. 16:25). Hence he calls himself a " dispenser of the mysteries of God " (1 Cor. 4:1). The essential is not the fine exposition, but the riches of the content of what is preached. And here he has proved his quality in every possible way to the Corinthians, and is in no way inferior to his opponents.

The Unremunerated Ministry (11:7–12)

7Or did I do wrong, when I humbled myself so that you could be exalted, as I preached the gospel of God to you without payment?

The opposition claimed it a proof of their superiority that St. Paul earned his living by the work of his hands, while they were supported by the community. And in fact, this principle of earning his own living set St. Paul apart from other missionaries. " Remember our toil and labor. We worked day and night, so as not to be a burden on any of you, while we preached the gospel of God to you " (1 Thess. 2:9). In 1 Corinthians he recalls that he would have the right to be supported by the community like other missionaries. But he says that he renounced this right in order not to hinder the gospel (1 Cor. 9:3–18). Nothing is said there about the Corinthians taking offense at the Apostle's attitude. But from 2 Corinthians we learn that he was criticized for it. This was, no doubt, a more recent development, promoted by his opponents, who must have claimed that St. Paul's conduct was a confession of his inferiority. Not being a true apostle, he had not enough confidence in himself to demand his support. He justifies himself with the ironic question as to whether this was some sort of sin. He describes his conduct as " humbling himself," which is to be taken quite literally. He had to earn his living by manual labor as a tentmaker, as the Acts of the Apostles tell us (18:3). Manual labor in antiquity was the task of slaves, and was despised accordingly. The double burden of being missionary and worker cost St. Paul very strenuous effort, and brought with it deprivation and poverty, and hence still further contempt (1 Cor. 4:11f.). His manual labor classed him among the witless and wretched: " We are homeless and wear ourselves out with the work of our hands " (1 Cor. 4:12f.). This is the humiliation which St. Paul undergoes to avoid burdening the Corinthians.

But through it they are " exalted." By the preaching of the Apostle, his apostolic ministry, and all his pastoral toils, they are saved instead of lost, children of God instead of sinners, rich instead of poor. Once hopelessly estranged from God, they are now with him (Eph. 2:13). They are no longer foreigners without civil rights among the people of God, but fellow citizens of the saints and members of the household of God (Eph. 2:19). To belong to the people and church of God is an exalted honor.

[8]*I despoiled other churches and took pay from them to be able to serve you . . .*

St. Paul explains how he could work in Corinth while accepting no monetary contributions from the community. He plundered other churches and had them pay for his services to Corinth.

These are military terms, which fit in with those used above, 10 : 3–5. Generals used to make conquered provinces pay the expenses of further campaigns. So too St. Paul. He had made almost violent requisitions in other churches for the sake of Corinth. This may have been in Macedonia and Athens, where St. Paul stayed before his first journey to Corinth, and Ephesus, where he worked before his later visits to Corinth.

The forcible terms are used to bring home to the Corinthians the fact that others made sacrifices on their behalf. But there is real truth behind them and they give us a glimpse of what happened in the early Christian and the Pauline missions. Stage by stage, the missions were extended. St. Paul considered new plans and discussed them with the existing churches where he was staying. At one stage the decision was taken to found a church at Corinth. St. Paul was ready to launch the venture and was to travel with some reliable helpers. Their travel expenses, their support, and the needs of a new church involved no little outlay. St. Paul worked hard to earn his own keep, but his personal needs were the least of the expenses. When new foundations were planned, money had to be collected in existing churches, and hence St. Paul could speak of requisitioning and even plundering.

[9]. . . *and when I was among you and was in want, I imposed on nobody. My needs were met by the brothers who came from Macedonia. And in all circumstances I avoided being a burden to you, as I shall continue to do in the future.*

But funds could run out and leave St. Paul himself in want. Even so, he was never a burden to anyone at Corinth. He was helped by the communities of Macedonia, such as those of

Thessalonica and Philippi. St. Paul was so confident of his warm relationships with the latter in particular that he accepted their aid without fear of provoking ill-will there. His letter to the Philippians includes an expression of gratitude for their help. They were the only ones at the time, he says, who " entered into fellowship with him in giving and receiving "; " not once but twice they supplied his needs " by sending contributions to him at Thessalonica (Phil. 4:15f.). But as for the Corinthians, St. Paul accepted nothing from them and will still refuse to do so.

[10]*As sure as the truth of Christ is in me, this is a boast which I shall never allow myself to be deprived of in the regions of Achaia.*

With still greater emphasis, St. Paul underlines what he has been saying by a sort of oath. He can swear that Christ speaks in him (13:3). Hence he can affirm that the truth of Christ is heard from his lips.

There will be no change in his attitude as regards being supported by the church. He regards it as a glory, of which he refuses to be deprived, at least throughout Achaia. Here he is avoiding exaggeration. He takes nothing in Achaia in the line of stipend for his ministry, that is, in Corinth, the capital of Achaia, he takes nothing for his ministry in Corinth. In other circumstances of a special nature he accepted help from Philippi.

[11]*Why? Because you are not dear to me? God knows that you are!*

In spite of his efforts to justify his conduct, he still hears the cry

of the church of Corinth, that it was only because he did not love
that church. His only answer is the brief assurance that God
knows the truth, that is, how much the Apostle loves the Corinthians. He seems to break off, under the stress of painful emotions and in a mood of resignation. What else can the loving
heart do when it is not believed and trusted in spite of all it says
and all the proofs it gives?

*12But what I have been doing I shall continue to do, to cut the
ground from under the feet of those who are looking for grounds
on which they can claim their boasts are as well-founded as mine.*

Though the Corinthians fail to understand him, St. Paul will
not alter his tactics. He knows that his opponents would like
him to, so that he would be no different from them. They boast
of being supported by the community, because they use this to
emphasize their dignity as apostles and it is a sign that the community acknowledges them as such. St. Paul, on the other hand,
by not asking for his keep, seems to admit that he is not a true
apostle. In this matter, on which they pride themselves so greatly,
they would like St. Paul to be as themselves. They would like all
apostles to be supported by the community in the same way. But
in point of fact they are well aware that St. Paul's disinterested-
ness puts him in a much more advantageous position. If he followed their line of conduct, he would no longer be a greater
apostle than they, and all would be equally well apostles. That is
why he refuses to fall in with their wishes. The difference is to
remain, to show everyone who wishes to see the truth, who is
the true apostle. It can only be he who serves not for his own
advantage, but for the good of the church.

The Pseudo-Apostles (11:13–15)

¹³*These people are pseudo-apostles, fraudulent workers, who have disguised themselves as apostles of Christ.*

The opposition call themselves apostles and claim the rights and status of apostles. They do not claim to belong to the college of the twelve, the old apostles, but they claim to be apostles in the wider sense. St. Paul's rejoinder, couched in very severe terms, is that they are not simply people whose weaknesses made them unworthy of their office, but that it is sheer presumption on their part to lay claim to the title and office of apostle. Angered and ruthless, St. Paul strips them of their pretensions. They are sham apostles, with no right to call themselves apostles. So far from being true missionaries of the gospel, they are frauds.

¹⁴*And no wonder. For Satan himself disguises himself as an angel of light.*

Such wickedness is so horrifying in the eyes of St. Paul that he can only explain it by Christ's mortal enemy, Satan, being at work. Like these sham apostles, Satan too likes to dress up and deceive. He too can appear in the form of an angel of light. His real nature is darkness (6:14f.). He is " ruler of the world of darkness " (Eph. 6:12). But the angels of God live in the radiant majesty of God and share in its brightness. Hence the true angels are angels of light, and the deceit is all the more brazen when Satan appears as an angel of light. We are reminded here of what our Lord said: " Beware of false prophets who come to you in sheep's clothing, but are ravening wolves within " (Mt. 7:15). False doctrine uses a veneer to sell its wares.

¹⁵*Hence there is nothing strange about his servants' disguising themselves as servants of righteousness. Their end will be in keeping with their works.*

The pseudo-apostles are the tools, envoys, and servants of Satan. He launches and directs their activities. The Apostle at any rate is convinced that Satan never ceases to try to hinder the apostolic mission with all the means at his disposal (2 : 11). " More than once we tried to come to you, but Satan prevented us " (1 Thess. 2 : 18).

St. Paul ends his vehement indictment with a threat of judgment. He ceases to refute them by argument and simply crushes them with a blow. By virtue of his supreme apostolic authority, he threatens the corrupters with God's judgment. The Apostle, like the whole church, is convinced that everyone will receive reward or punishment according to his works (5 : 10).

Another Request for Patience with Paul's Boasting (11 : 16–21)

¹⁶*Once more I ask: let no one take me for a fool. But if I am taken for a fool, accept me even on these terms, and allow me to boast a little.*

St. Paul returns to his request for a patient hearing, even if he speaks as a fool (11 : 1). Going beyond his announcement there, he now explains that his folly will take the form of boastful praise of himself. He starts, however, by making a request in the contrary direction: no one is to take him for a fool. He finds it so repugnant to appear as a fool that he begs not to be taken

for one. But if in the end, compelled by his opponents, he boasts
like a fool, even then the Corinthians must bear with him and
accept him on these terms. For the sake of his apostolic office,
Paul has to speak of himself. But even so he cannot find it in his
heart to speak seriously. Hence he must dress up his words in cap
and bells, much as he dislikes it.

*17What I say [now], is not said according to the Lord, but as it
were in folly, in this attitude of boasting.*

He also knows that such talk is not according to the Lord. To
boast is to act contrary to the example given by Christ. He has
said that Christ, being rich, became poor for the sake of men
(8:9). He has presented him as the example of meekness and
gentleness (10:1). What he knows about the Lord is that he was
in the form of God, but that he emptied himself and took the
form of man and humbled himself by becoming obedient even
unto death (Phil. 2:5–9). "Christ did not live for his own
pleasure, but took upon himself [on the cross] the reproaches
which were directed against God " (Rom. 15:3).

*18Since there are so many who boast according to the flesh, I
will also boast.*

St. Paul baulks again and again at starting to speak like a fool.
He finds it unattractive and in fact senseless, even when it is
forced upon him. But many do it, and what many do, he has to
copy. The many in question are men in general, but especially
his opponents at Corinth who boast of their privileges and
thereby gain adherents. It is, of course, a line of action not
according to the Lord but according to the flesh. Flesh means

here natural and unredeemed man, not transformed by the Spirit, and strictly speaking sinful man who prizes his own privileges and tries to gain standing and power through self-praise.

¹⁹For you gladly bear with fools, prudent as you are. ²⁰You bear with it if someone enslaves you, if someone devours you, if someone overreaches you, if someone lords it over you, if someone hits you in the face.

The indignant Apostle has recourse to harsh words. He calls his opponents fools, because their boasting has made them such. But how patient are the Corinthians with these fools, and how gladly they put up with them! With pointed irony, he calls the Corinthians prudent, since they think they are so wise and yet let themselves be hoodwinked.

In five parallel phrases, each as sharp as a whiplash, St. Paul lays bare this prudence of the Corinthians for what it is worth. They accept everything and put up with everything without seeing that they are being deceived. They do not notice that they are being brought under the yoke by the sham apostles, who impose laws and precepts on them and rob them of the freedom of the redeemed. The Corinthians are being exploited, indeed devoured, since these tricksters demand their support from them. The Corinthians are being attacked and captured, since they are allowing themselves to be dragged in the wake of the sham apostles. And they do not notice the haughtiness of these men by whom they are being overwhelmed. They let themselves be slapped in the face, be coarsely insulted, and be the victims of all sorts of violence. St. Paul hurls grave accusations against his opponents in order to open the eyes of the Corinthians. Not only do these men preach a false gospel (11:4) but they are arrogant and overbearing, and strike down ruthlessly all opposition. Their one object is to exploit the community for their own benefit.

21I am ashamed to admit it, but we have been too weak to do such things. —But where anybody can be bold (I say this in my folly), there I can be bold too.

The short sentence with which St. Paul concludes his list of charges against his opponents is so terse that the explanation is uncertain. He means, no doubt, that he must admit it to his shame that he, at any rate, is too weak to do violence to the community as his opponents have done. This would then once more be ironical. What he brands as his shame is, of course, his unselfish service. But the Corinthians do not recognize where the truth lies.

With this St. Paul feels that he has excused and justified himself sufficiently. It is now time to begin to speak like a fool in praise of himself. He is only acting like the others whom the Corinthians regard favorably, no matter what they do.

Earthly and Heavenly Boasts of Paul (11 : 22—12 : 10)

HARDSHIPS AND SUFFERING (11 :22–33)

22They are Hebrews? So am I. They are Israelites? So am I. They are the children of Abraham? So am I.

St. Paul at last begins to praise himself like a fool. The discourse is in two parts, dealing in 11 : 22–33 with things of earth and human matters, in 12 : 1–10 with divine and heavenly revelations.

The exposition proceeds along the same lines as other catalogs in which St. Paul lists the hardships of his ministry. But this speech is the most closely-packed, comprehensive, and passionate of them all, charged with powerful emotions and sweeping all before it in a torrent of excitement. It is natural eloquence inspired by genuine feeling, but it makes use of the forms and formulas of a cultured diction.

In 11:22f., St. Paul contrasts himself with his opponents, dealing point by point with what they affirm and what he himself really is. But in 11:24-33 he drops such comparisons. He disregards his opponents and confines himself to his own history with its mass of sufferings and labors.

He begins with the external privileges on which his opponents pride themselves, their ancestry and noble birth. Having heard the opposition claiming such advantages, he retorts vigorously that in such matters he is in no way their inferior but rather their superior.

The three claims to a privileged position by reason of birth— Hebrews, Israelites, children of Abraham—are not just elegant variation. Each word has a specific meaning. " Hebrews " is the word used to designate the people or race which by descent, faith, language, and customs was distinct from other peoples (Gen. 11:14). It indicates racial purity, the pure blood in the veins which the Jews preserved with such care and pride. " Israel " (" the fighter for God ") is the name which God him- self conferred on the patriarch Jacob (Gen. 32:28). The name includes the promises to Israel, its hopes and expectations, as well as the certainty of belonging to the chosen people. "Abraham " is the father of Israel and bearer of the great messianic promises (Gen. 15:5). To belong to the " seed of Abraham " was the guarantee by which a share in the future messianic blessings was

assured. The fact that the opposition claimed such privileges
shows that they were genuine Jews. Nonetheless, in their own
way they preached Christ and the gospel (11 : 4). Hence St. Paul's
opponents are Christians who have come from Judaism and are
proud of their Judaism.

St. Paul does not fall short of his opponents as regards purity
and nobility of Jewish blood. He can show at times clearly
enough that he is a loyal Jew who is proud of his descent from
Abraham. He points with pride to the fact that he can trace his
ancestry to Benjamin, one of the twelve sons of Jacob, and thus
to the holy patriarchs of Israel. " I am an Israelite, of the seed
of Abraham, of the tribe of Benjamin " (Rom. 11 : 1). " If anyone thinks that he can have confidence in the flesh, I can do so
far more. I was circumcised on the eighth day, I am from the
race of Israel, from the tribe of Benjamin, a Hebrew of the
Hebrews " (Phil. 3 : 4f.). But these are all fleshly prerogatives,
which are now worthless, and even harmful, in the order of
salvation brought by Christ. It is for this reason that St. Paul
must now oppose the false gospel and the baneful demands of
the Judaizers.

[23]*They are servants of Christ? I speak as though I had lost my
wits—so am I, but far more. In far more labors, in far more
prisons, under countless blows, in mortal straits many times.*

Along with the prerogatives of birth, the opposition claim
another proud title, that of " servants of Christ." They did not
mean this in the sense in which it could be said of any Christian.
They meant that they were servants of Christ in a special way,
being apostles in the service of the mission and so of the Lord.
The point had come up shortly before (11 : 15), and St. Paul

had denied them the right to this title, branding them instead as servants of Satan. Here he does not examine their title deeds, but declares that he has far more right to the title of servant of Christ. And now he is no longer content to point out and establish his equality. He affirms his superiority to all his opponents, though he does not fail to insert one last excuse for his boasting: he is delirious!

But even with regard to the twelve first apostles St. Paul can affirm: " I have worked far harder than any of them " (1 Cor. 15:10). This is a statement which he can prove to the hilt against the false apostles of Corinth. He begins by mentioning, in four parallel phrases, typical situations which recurred again and again, in which he proved himself a steadfast servant of Christ: the labors of missionary work, imprisonment (6:5), court proceedings in which evidence was taken under the lash (11:24f.), and finally mortal danger (1:9f.; 4:11). These four headings are then illustrated by further details of the sufferings and dangers of St. Paul's ministry.

²⁴*By the Jews I was five times given forty [strokes of the lash] less one.*

This is the beginning of a long enumeration of events in the life of the missionary Apostle. The arrangement is difficult to follow. St. Paul clearly does not follow the chronological sequence, but groups together similar types of events. First come some painful experiences which can be counted exactly and with figures. St. Paul starts with the scourgings inflicted on him five times by Jewish authorities. Thus the Jews are named first and foremost. The Jewish authorities proceeded on the basis of scripture when inflicting the punishment of forty lashes minus one: " Forty

strokes may be given, but not more " (Deut. 25:3). To make sure
of not breaking the law by a miscount, only thirty-nine strokes
were given. Jewish accounts of the punishment say that the
criminal was tied to a post and beaten with leather thongs. The
punishment was not merely cruel—it could sometimes be fatal—
it was also extremely ignominious. And St. Paul's body, which
had to endure these severe beatings, was that of a man in ill-
health (12:7). The Jews imposed such penalties on teachers of
false doctrine, and hence on St. Paul, presumably because he
preached that the crucified was the Messiah and because he
asserted that salvation was bestowed on all men, gentiles as well
as Jews, that Israel had lost its privileges and that the Old Testament law was no longer in force.

*25Three times was I flogged, once stoned, three times did I suffer
shipwreck, a night and a day passed while I was [tossed about]
in the sea.*

Three further floggings are recalled apart from those inflicted by
the Jewish authorities. They must have been ordered by the
Roman authorities, possibly on the charge of having caused
breaches of the peace. One case is recorded in the Acts of the
Apostles, the flogging of the Apostle and his companion Silas in
Philippi.

The stoning is probably also the one recorded in Acts 14:19,
which tells how St. Paul was stoned by the mob at Lystra, at the
instigation of the Jews. A stoning usually resulted in death, as
in the case of Stephen (Acts 7:60). And at Lystra, St. Paul was
dragged unconscious out of the town and left for dead.

None of the three shipwrecks are mentioned at all by the Acts
of the Apostles. (The one off Malta [Acts 27:9–44] took place

some years after the writing of the second letter to the Corinthians.) We cannot say when these shipwrecks took place, on
journeys recorded in Acts or on quite different ones. In this connection St. Paul mentions an occasion when his life was in the
utmost danger as he was tossed about for many long hours in
the open sea.

*[26]On many journeys, in dangers from rivers, dangers from high-
waymen, dangers from men of my own race, dangers from gentiles, dangers in the city, dangers in the wilderness, dangers
among false brethren.*

The enumeration continues with the dangers undergone by St.
Paul on his journeys from mission to mission. Like 11:27, there
is no finite verb in the sentence. It must be supplied from 11:23.
" As servant of Christ I have proved myself . . ." The dangers,
underlined by the word being repeated eight times, are partly
such as beset every traveler in antiquity, partly such as St. Paul
had to run as messenger of the gospel.

Fording rivers and wading through them could be dangerous,
especially after heavy rains. St. Paul must have had to cross
many large rivers, especially when traveling in Asia Minor.

Apart from dangers in the wilds of nature, St. Paul was also
threatened by men. First he names the highwaymen, and then
the traps set for him as a Christian missionary. He had to suffer
the onslaughts of Jews, gentiles, and Christians. He has just
mentioned the menace of floggings and stoning by Jews, but
there were others, including charges brought against him before
the Roman authorities, mob violence incited by the Jews, life
made impossible for him in city after city. The dangers from
the gentiles or pagans have already been signaled by the three

floggings which he suffered, but he was also threatened with arrest, criminal charges, and the like. (In the end he was beheaded by the Romans at the side of the road leading from Rome to Ostia.) But even within the communities which he founded, he was exposed to danger from false brethren. Such attacks were all the more dangerous because St. Paul suspected nothing, and perhaps was unable to see for a long time in what quarter danger was lurking. He means, no doubt, the pseudo-apostles, who were "false brethren" or fellow Christians, as has just been described. But there were also the difficulties which beset him from the side of fanatical Jewish Christians in Jerusalem (Acts 21 : 20–22) and the fierce onslaughts of extremist Jewish Christians in such places as Galatia, where they demanded that even gentile Christians should adopt the Jewish way of life (Gal. 2 : 4; 5 : 12; 6 : 3). The struggle with such adversaries was hard. St. Paul had constantly to defend himself against attacks, calumnies, and efforts to displace him. Possibly they went so far as to threaten his life at times.

St. Paul then groups three dangers according to locality : in the city, in the desert, on the high seas. These have already been indicated from different aspects.

²⁷*In toil and labor, in night-long vigils, in hunger and thirst, in many fasts, in cold and exposure.*

These hardships and deprivations were also imposed on St. Paul by his service of the gospel. He had to go without sleep, partly because he was forced to give his nights to pastoral work, since he worked for his living in the daytime, partly because his anxieties robbed him of sleep. Hunger, thirst, and fasts were not acts of self-denial voluntarily chosen, but often enough simply the deprivations of a man left penniless, or again, those of a hunted man or a convict. The uncomfortable conditions under which he traveled exposed him to extremes of heat and cold. His overland journeys must have been mostly on foot, the ordinary means of transport being beyond his means. He was too poor to avail himself of the facilities then provided, though his opponents did not hesitate to batten on the communities (11:20).

²⁸*Along with all the rest, the pressures on me every day, my anxieties for all the churches.*

St Paul finally mentions the burdens of his actual apostolic vocation. The pressures which he experienced every day came both from men and things. Men flocked to him and demanded his attention: Christians who needed counsel and consolation, a word of encouragement or warning; pagans who sought further instruction; querulous Jews or Christians to trouble him with their complaints. He was also under pressure from circumstances and events, the endless difficulties which pressed upon him from all sides, sometimes deliberately provoked by his adversaries.

Along with the pastoral cares of the local churches where the Apostle was staying at the moment, there were also the anxieties imposed on him by the communities which he had founded and whose progress he had to guide. All the churches kept him tense and watchful. He would have liked to be everywhere at the same time. Mostly all he could do was to try to help by messengers and letters. He bore a truly ecumenical burden, which grew heavier every day. What did his jaundiced opponents in Corinth know of all this? How many even of his friends knew about it?

²⁹Who is weak and I am not weak? Where does anyone fall that I am not inflamed?

Having spoken of the extent and number of his cares, St. Paul now speaks of their gravity and intensity. His comprehensive care for the whole church throughout the world also means sharing the experiences and the troubles of each Christian. He bears each of them in his heart, troubled for them, praying for them (Phil. 1 : 7). He suffers birth pangs in the process of making Christians of them (Gal. 4 : 19). He rejoices with those who rejoice, is sad with those who are sad (Rom. 12 : 15). He suffers anguish at the fall and ruin of every sinner. " To the weak he became weak " (1 Cor. 9 : 22). If someone is misled and ultimately falls into sin, St. Paul himself cannot fail to be inflamed with compassion, pain, and dread, and no doubt with anger, though he was always willing to help and heal.

³⁰If there must be boasting, then I will boast of my weakness. ³¹The God and Father of the Lord Jesus, blessed be his name for ever, knows that I do not lie.

St. Paul concludes this part of his panegyric by justifying and excusing his folly once more. Since boasting is the order of the day, St. Paul joins in. But what he boasts of is the direct opposite of the arrogant presumption of his opponents and their glorification of their privileges and achievements. His boast is of his weakness. What he has narrated is no doubt a revelation of the Apostle's strength and endurance. But it is also a description of his weakness, since it shows the permanent insufficiency of human forces. And it is under this latter aspect that St. Paul is now speaking of it. He is a man unprotected and powerless, exposed to all sorts of hindrances and obstacles from within and without, to all sorts of dangers from the forces of nature and the wickedness of men. Along with his own disabilities he has to take on the burden of those of his fellow Christians. Hence it has been a description of his weakness. And his attitude is precisely the opposite of that of his adversaries in Corinth, who insist on their privileges and accomplishments. No doubt St. Paul also recognizes that there is a true pride to be taken in weakness, since there the power of God is revealed as with him, supporting him and confirming him publicly before the church and the world when he has not broken down under his weakness. There is a hint of this here, and he finally affirms roundly that the power of God shows itself at the most perfect in weakness (12:9).

St. Paul affixes his seal to the story of his woes by asseverating that his proud words were absolutely true. Once more, as in 1:23, he swears by the God and Father of Jesus, and adds a doxology in praise of God.

[32]*At Damascus, the governor appointed by King Aretas kept the city under watch, to seize my person,* [33]*and I was let down in a basket through a window in the wall, and so escaped his hands.*

These two verses are obviously an epilogue to the panegyric. This had been in a series of terse phrases with well marked rhythms in a quick and lively movement, but the epilogue is expansive and prosaic and gives exact names and places. St. Paul's escape from Damascus is also narrated in the Acts of the Apostles (Acts 9:24). Aretas IV, King of the Nabataeans, 9 B.C. to A.D. 40, then held Damascus, which he governed by a legate. With the Jews urging him on, the governor tried to arrest St.

Paul, but he slipped through his hands by having himself lowered through a window of a house, which must have stood on the outer wall. This episode must have come very vividly to his mind as he dictated his list of hardships. He used it as a special instance of the dangers which had threatened his life and added it in to close the list.

VISIONS AND REVELATIONS (12: 1–9a)

12:1Boasting is in order. It is futile. Nevertheless, I will come to the visions and revelations granted me by the Lord.

12: 1–9a is the second part of the Apostle's self-praise. It forms a contrast to the first part (11:22–33) which spoke of earthly privileges, but above all of toil, suffering, and weakness which were the Apostle's lot (11:23–33). But now he turns to the extraordinary heavenly revelations with which God favored him. But even this becomes a praise of weakness, since here too St. Paul affirms that these graces were given to a man suffering from infirmities, so that here too the power of God was effective in the midst of weakness. Thus the two parts of the discourse come to the same conclusion.

Once more he affirms that he only praises himself under compulsion. He knows that it is useless. Existence as a Christian, existence in the Lord is not helped thereby (11:17). Nonetheless, he speaks of his visions and revelations, openly for once, though only because he is forced to. Elsewhere he only hints at his visions and revelations, in a few passages in his letters. He says, for instance, that he has received revelations about the final salvation of Israel, his own people (Rom. 11:25), about the mystery of the resurrection of the dead at the end of time (1 Cor. 15:51), and about the return of Christ (1 Thess. 4:15). He speaks again and again of the apparition of the glorified Christ which was accorded to him on the way to Damascus. The Acts of the Apostles records other mysterious visions.

²*I know of a man in Christ, that fourteen years ago—whether in the body I do not know or outside the body I do not know, but God knows—the man in question was caught up as far as the third heaven.*

In a very peculiar, solemn, and mysterious style, St. Paul speaks of the overwhelming experience of an ascension into heaven which he had fourteen years before. Important elements remain unsaid or mysterious, such as where it happened, how he was taken up, what he saw, the revelations which he heard and the manner of his return to earth. It is a mystery from which the veil is only half lifted. He shudders as he speaks of it. Much of it remained hidden from himself. " I do not know," he admits. What he tells, he tells only under compulsion, in order to defend his office. The rest of what he experienced he leaves untold because they are God's secrets of which he may not speak, and also because human speech is incapable of expressing them (12:4).

He seems not to be speaking of himself but of someone he knows, " a man in Christ." The reason why he uses this form of narrative will be explained later: " On account of the man in question I will boast. But of myself I refuse to boast " (12:5). This is a confession that no personal merit of his own has given rise to this experience, of which he was completely unworthy. Hence he does not say " I," but speaks of a " man in Christ."

The subject of the experience was not the earthly, natural man, but the Christian redeemed and sanctified in Christ.

The date is precise, fourteen years before. It was an extraordinary experience, which was stamped on his memory as something unique. Even such a saint as Paul was granted such experiences only very rarely, and they were by no means within his reach at all times. What remain constant are only the labors and infirmities to which he almost succumbs. Ecstasy is the exception and not the shape and style of his life in Christ.

While affirming his ignorance of the manner in which he was rapt to heaven and of his perceptions, he says that he was no doubt taken up in one of the two possible forms of such ascensions into heaven, either in the body, that is, the whole man, soul and body, or outside the body, that is, that the soul alone ascended while the body remained on earth. Ancient writings, especially some from the Judaism of the time, tell us that journeys to heaven were represented as taking place in either of these two ways, and that favored individuals had been so taken up. Hence St. Paul is drawing on concepts familiar in his day to recount and explain, both to himself and others, his extraordinary experiences. What he is certain of beyond all question is that he had experienced a very great grace. " God knows " how it all took place. This God is the Apostle's guarantee of the truth and reality of his journey to heaven. He appeals to God as witness when he speaks of it.

The mention of the " third heaven " and of " paradise " is also in keeping with Jewish ideas of the time. Jewish theology then assumed that there were a number of heavens, one above the other—three, five, seven, or ten in number. The lowest was the heaven of the atmosphere, then came the heaven in which the stars moved, and higher still the heaven in which the blessed, the angels, and finally God dwelt. In accordance with the world picture of his times, St. Paul speaks of the third heaven, which for him must have meant the supreme and highest. He does not explain how he knew that he was in the third heaven. Possibly this was matter of a revelation. Possibly he only assumed it, in keeping precisely with the mental images and calculations of his day.

³And I know of the man in question—whether in the body or outside the body I do not know, but God knows—⁴ᵃthat he was taken up into paradise . . .

Using the same words as before, St. Paul describes once more his journey to heaven. We cannot be certain whether the two parallel narratives mean the same journey or two different ones. Though the twofold description could suggest two different events, it is assumed to be more probable that he is speaking of the same happening. Both descriptions are given under the same date, "fourteen years ago." In St. Paul's day, it was thought that after the fall af Adam, paradise had been raised from earth to heaven, and was now in the third heaven as the place of bliss. St. Paul seems to be following this idea when he indicates that his journey had taken him to the third heaven or into paradise. Dwelling on the journey in this way, with two descriptions of it, was therefore meant to express the greatness of the experience.

⁴ᵇ. . . and heard unutterable words, which human lips may not speak.

St. Paul gives no description of what he saw in heaven. Contemporary Jewish narratives of journeys to heaven, however, are very profuse in their descriptions, as the curiosity of their readers demanded. St. Paul is significantly different, not trying to indulge curiosity and fantasy. He only says that he heard words, but that he cannot impart them, since they are forbidden to human lips. They are mysteries of God which may not be revealed before the due time. But to have been initiated into them is a supreme moment in the life of the Apostle and a privilege which he shares with no one else. It is his supreme title to boast, which is why he speaks of it now.

But here he breaks off. He says nothing about his descent from heaven, about coming to himself, or about how he felt after the journey, where comparable writings of the time are again profuse. Once more, he refuses to pander to curiosity.

He describes his experiences in mental images such as the culture of his day supplied, and which he had used as a rabbinical theologian to construct his own world picture and world of ideas. He shows that he himself senses the uncertainty and fragility of his description, by repeating so often, " I do not know," " God knows." Men always think and speak in terms of the ideas of their times, as we still do today. Insofar as St. Paul uses such contemporary concepts and patterns, he is not giving them the certainty of revelation and faith. Nonetheless, using the language of his time, he describes an event which was to him a supreme revelation. We have no experience of such things and cannot therefore follow them. But neither have we the right to make the contents of our consciousness and our capacity for experience the standard of all things in heaven and on earth. And hence we have not the right to maintain that St. Paul's experience, while very mysterious and strange, was still a natural psychological phenomenon. He is convinced and he knows that he experienced a supreme gift of divine grace. What form it took, as St. Paul himself says, God knows.

⁵On account of the man in question I will boast, but not of myself, except that I boast of my weaknesses.

The special circumstances forced St. Paul to speak of these things. They were a supreme privilege. But he does not boast about himself. He accords the glory to that other person who is the recipient of graces. He does not praise himself, but the grace of the Lord, and the Lord who was supremely powerful in him. When he speaks of himself, he continues to say that he has nothing to boast of but his weakness.

After a stubborn resistance and only under compulsion, St. Paul disclosed for once his great experiences. Elsewhere he never spoke of them. They are private revelations on which the church cannot be founded and which cannot be used to build it up. They are not the gospel of Christ and hence not what is preached in the church. Should it not always hold good that visionary and ecstatic experiences, being personal graces, are not to be preached in the church?

⁶If I do decide to boast, it will not be folly, for I shall be speaking the truth. But I renounce the undertaking, so that no one may think more of me than what he sees or hears from me, even in view of the superabundance of revelations.

St. Paul refuses to boast, though he could point to special graces and revelations. Is he referring to the journey to heaven which he has described or other revelations of which he is unwilling to speak further? But even if he did boast, he would be telling the truth. However, he renounces the idea. He does not want to be judged except on the basis of ordinary things, his actions and his utterances which can be seen and heard by everyone. He does not wish the extraordinary things, one of which he has just recounted, to be " credited to his account " (the literal sense of the Greek). They are not to be taken into account when people come in contact with him and pass judgment on his person. He does not wish to wear the halo of a higher being, of a pious and saintly personage, much less that of a man who has once been to heaven. All this is a secret between the Apostle and God, and it is to remain so.

⁷Therefore, to prevent my growing arrogant, I was given a thorn in the flesh, an angel of Satan, to pound me with his fists, so that I should not grow arrogant.

St. Paul has the highest graces. But even this privileged person, and precisely because he is privileged, is subjected by God to discipline, to prevent his being over-elated. The discipline which God imposes on St. Paul takes the form of grave suffering. St. Paul speaks of it in veiled terms. According to the most prevalent interpretation, it is an illness which sapped his strength and humiliated him.

He begins with a metaphor drawn from ordinary life. He feels his bodily suffering like a thorn or goad which continually pricks and torments his body. Or does the striking metaphor mean that he felt his illness like a stake in the flesh? The cruel punishment of impaling on a stake was sometimes inflicted in antiquity. Does St. Paul mean that his whole life is like that of a man impaled on a stake or turnspit?

The other image uses mythological words and concepts. St. Paul's sickness makes him feel as if he were being hammered and beaten to the ground by Satan's fists. He says very often that

Satan is hindering his mission. Satan had his helpers in this work, such as are listed for instance in the letter to the Ephesians as " the principalities, powers, and rulers of this world " (Eph. 6:12). St. Paul's view coincides with the general notion of the Bible that illnesses are the work of Satan. In the great Old Testament epic of the Book of Job, Satan is allowed to strike Job with leprosy (Job 2:6f.). Jesus himself says of a woman who had had a stoop for eighteen years that Satan has bound this daughter of Abraham (Lk. 13:16). This is based on the knowledge and insight given by faith that God is creator and giver of life. But illness and death are the collapse and destruction of life. God, the Lord of life, cannot himself be the destroyer of it. Hence illness and death do not come from him but are the work of the universal destroyer, Satan.

God permitted and still permits Satan to strike St. Paul with illness. " I was given it," says St. Paul. God gave it. Satan is not an absolute despot; he must serve God's purposes and plans. The work of the Apostle was gravely hindered by the feebleness of his body. But this was to keep this highly privileged Apostle from thinking proudly that his own powers made him equal to any task.

It is very remarkable that St. Paul uses such very different ways of describing his illness. First he uses a metaphor from everyday life, and then he brings in weighty assertions about God and Satan. He finds both types of description equally valid. He does not think them essentially different, while our critical exegesis today makes a distinction, such as between the natural and the mythological interpretation. Both ways of speaking are metaphorical and figurative for St. Paul, and he does not insist on their being taken literally and word for word. In either case, the diction is not a matter of faith. But the conviction thereby expressed by St. Paul is a truth of faith, namely, that even evil is subordinated to God's plan and must serve salvation. As he says elsewhere: " For those who love God, all things work for good " (Rom. 8 : 28).

8Three times I prayed to the Lord about it, asking that it should leave me.

Simply and movingly, St. Paul tells of the prayer sent up three times for the removal of the suffering which weighed him down. He has something more to narrate than the continual patience with which he bore his illness. He also remembers clearly how he struggled in prayer and cried out three times. He either made the same petition three times in succession in the course of a prayer, or asked for help on three different occasions. He asked what was the meaning of his affliction and hence struggled to understand the burden. He stormed heaven with prayers, asking Christ to help his Apostle against Satan. Twice there was no answer. Only to his third prayer was an answer given.

He called three times upon the Lord. Who is this Lord? It is probably not simply God, as the word might mean, but the Lord Christ. St. Paul often gives Christ the title of " Lord," which indicates his divine majesty. According to the gospels, Christ is the stronger man who invades the house of the strong man (Satan) and binds him (Mt. 12: 29). The redemptive work of Christ conquered Satan and his helpers (Col. 2: 15). So here too this Christ is asked to answer St. Paul's prayer and utter a word of command to the angel of Satan.

This tells us that St. Paul and the church prayed to Christ. We do this spontaneously. But it was not so obvious from the beginning in the New Testament. On principle, the prayer of the church is directed to the heavenly Father. But even in the New Testament the church already begins to pray also to Christ, thereby attesting its belief that he is the Lord in divine majesty and power. Christians are accordingly described as those " who call on the name of the Lord Jesus Christ " (Acts 9:14). And St. Paul himself describes the church as the fellowship of those " who call on the name of our Lord Jesus Christ " (1 Cor. 1:2).

⁹ᵃ*And he said to me: " My grace is enough for you. Power is most fully developed in weakness."*

Christ's answer to the prayer of St. Paul was equivalent to a refusal. The answer was: You need nothing more than the power of grace, and that you have. The banishment of the angel of Satan is superfluous.

Divine grace acts in man as a force, which is all the more apparent and complete in its action, the weaker the man in whom it acts. For it is at the moment when man is clearly impotent that one can see that divine power, not human strength, is at work. It was better, therefore, that St. Paul should remain in a state of weakness. The grace of God only comes to its full strength in the weakness of the Apostle, which is precisely where it is best shown.

St. Paul has to say in one breath, as it were, that he is united in marvelous sublimity with the heavenly world and that he is abandoned in painful impotence to the Satanic power which causes his suffering. He sees the divine mysteries and receives unutterable messages, while reeling under the blows of Satan's angel. His life bridges the loftiest heights and the lowest depths, which brings an almost unbearable tension into his whole life and ministry. But he understands that this must be so if he is

to remain the servant of Christ, preserved from religious pride
and empty boast. His sufferings and the buffetings of the angel
of Satan do not separate him from his Lord and his grace. In
spite of everything, the Apostle remains in Christ. Weakness in
fact is where the power of the Lord is most fully effective and
manifest, as the Lord tells him explicitly. The experience of the
Apostle remains a model for all the Christian life of faith.

POWER IN WEAKNESS (12:9b–10)

[9b]*Hence I shall boast much more gladly of my weaknesses, so
that the power of Christ may come upon me.*

In response to the words of the Lord, St. Paul reaffirms his desire
to boast of his weakness. His assertion takes on a new depth
and force from what he has related in the meantime of his
experience of divine force in human impotence. He will gladly
boast of his weakness, which means renouncing all desire to
be freed of his burden. He is confident that weakness is always
filled with divine force. God's power and grace are not given
definitively at a given moment, once and for all time, but are
a never-ending succession of events in which truth and salvation
are bestowed anew on man. This gives that assurance of victory
which is so often on the lips of St. Paul: " It is no longer I
who live, but Christ who lives in me " (Gal. 2:20), or, " I
can do all in him who strengthens me " (Phil. 4:13).

[10]*Hence I am happy for the sake of Christ in weaknesses, under
ill-treatment, in want, in persecutions, and in straits. For when
I am weak, then I am strong.*

Once more St. Paul gives a little catalog of sufferings, which recalls his earlier and more comprehensive lists. The catalog explains what is meant by weaknesses. The mention of ill-treatment recalls his experiences at the hands of unjust judges; the persecutions recall the enormities committed by Jews, Christians, and pagans; want and straits of various kinds recall the sufferings heaped so abundantly upon him.

Finally (12:10b), he repeats the truth taught by the words of the Lord (12:9a). The principle is of universal validity, but here it appears in the first person singular as the Apostle's own profession of faith. Thus St. Paul submitted himself joyfully and without reserve to the truth imparted by his Lord, and made God's word and will the basis and rule of his life.

The Signs of the Apostle (12:11–13)

[11]*I have been a fool. You forced me to it. I should really have been commended by you. For I am in no way inferior to the super-apostles, even though I am nothing.*

The fool's speech is ended. St. Paul takes off the cap and bells and behaves naturally. He explains and excuses his behavior once more. He was forced into it by the Corinthians. Once more he takes up the main point of his defense, his equality with the super-apostles. He falls short of them at no point. But here he adds, speaking in the most trenchant way possible, that he is nothing. This may be taken as a last and most profound confession of his weakness, true in the sense that he is nothing in the sight of God's judgment. But it could also be a verdict which St. Paul, with bitter irony, attributes to the Corinthians.

¹²The signs of the Apostle were performed among you, in all patience, through signs and wonders and mighty works.

St. Paul gives a new proof of the authenticity of his apostolic office, the apostolic signs which he wrought in Corinth. He distinguishes them as " signs," " wonders," and " mighty works." All three words are New Testament expressions for miracles. It is hardly possible to say how St. Paul exactly distinguished them. But the use of three words brings out the great number of feats which he was able to perform. In the letter to the Romans —written at Corinth—St. Paul also speaks of what Christ wrought through him " for the conversion of the gentiles, through words and deeds, through the power of signs and wonders, through the power of the Spirit " (Rom. 15:18f.). In 1 Corinthians, he lists the gifts of the Spirit in mighty works which God brings about in the church " distributing them to each as he wills." They include " words of wisdom, words of knowledge, faith, power to heal, prophecy, discernment of spirits, the gift of tongues," which are not all miracles in the strict sense which we usually attach to the word (1 Cor 12:4–11). What does St. Paul mean in the present text? Perhaps inspired preaching, marvelous conversions, reconciliations, healings of illness, and the like.

The New Testament writers know that unbelief is curious about miracles but is not converted even by the greatest miracles. Hence miracles are not granted to unbelief. But where there is a genuine will to believe, the gospel is demonstrated by miracles, and the good will is granted miracles (Jn. 20:30). In this way, miracles are among the valid criteria of the Apostle, and are among the proofs and proprieties of the apostolic office. Hence St. Paul appeals to the miracles which he wrought in Corinth.

According to the gospels, it is certain that Jesus, by virtue of his authority to perform mighty works and miracles, also gave his disciples the power and the mission to do similar works: " And he called the twelve to himself and gave them power over the unclean spirits, to drive them out, and to heal all illness and infirmity " (Mt. 10:1). The words and the command of the Lord, accepted in faith, gave the disciples power over illnesses and the forces of destruction. It is not a magical power. It is effective only through prayer, hence in the union of faith with God, as one of our Lord's sayings puts it: " This type of demon cannot be driven out except by prayer " (Mk. 9:29). And the power of performing miracles is not the most important thing. The fellowship and love of God are more important still: " Do not rejoice that the demons have been subjected to you. Rejoice rather that your names are written in heaven " (Lk. 10:20).

With the confidence of faith, the church of the apostles took up the struggle with the destructive forces working against body and soul. The church is certain that " the prayer of faith will save the sick man, and the Lord will raise him up " (Jas. 5:15). The Acts of the Apostles recounts miraculous deeds in which the apostles helped and healed many. Perspectives of the history of the church's mission, as already given in the New Testament, also envisage the same type of happening. St. Paul too was conscious of having the power to work signs and wonders. This does not mean that he had magical powers. When his loyal helper Epaphroditus was mortally ill, it never occurred to St. Paul to perform a miraculous cure. He prayed instead for God's mercy and consolation, and then thanked him when the sick man grew better (Phil. 2:26). The natural order of things remains. But within it God does miracles which only faith recognizes. The church cannot call on miraculous powers which would turn the world into a fabulously beautiful and splendid place. " All patience " still remains necessary, since it is the power to bear and suffer all that time and the world bring.

[13]*What were you deprived of more than the other churches, except that I myself was not a burden to you? Pardon me this fault!*

St. Paul had displayed the full force of his apostolic ministry at Corinth. The church there had had to go short of nothing that the other churches had, except one thing. St. Paul had accepted nothing for his own support, as he affirms again (cf. 11 : 9) with bitter irony. He was not a burden on the Corinthians. He did not exploit them for his own benefit. If that was an injustice, they must forgive him.

INFORMATION AND FINAL EXHORTATIONS
(12:14—13:10)

To end his letter, St. Paul announces another visit, which will be his third (12:4; 13:1), and adds some warnings in view of this visit. This final section, as usual, also includes information about his further plans. But the Apostle's personal apologia also continues to the end of the letter, with his sentences constantly running into each other.

Paul's Visit in the Near Future (12:14)

14Well then, I am now ready to come to you for the third time, and I shall not be a burden. I do not seek your goods but your-selves. For children have not to save for their parents, but parents for their children.

St. Paul announces his third visit to Corinth. But he returns at once to his defense of himself, explaining once more why he refused to claim his support from the community. Having already said that he wished to be a burden on nobody and that he would not use his office for personal gain (11:9; 12:13), he emphasizes once more that he is not aiming at the Corinthians' goods and chattels, but at their own persons and their salvation. Then he gives another reason for his behavior by appealing to a principle generally admitted in ordinary life. All parents work and save for their children, not children for their parents. The reference to the natural order of things is apt and convincing, because when speaking of his relationship to the community, St. Paul often says that he is its father. Under these circumstances, it would be actually unnatural for St. Paul to have himself supported by the church.

Paul's Self-Sacrifice (12:15–18)

[15]*But I will gladly make sacrifices, and indeed be sacrificed for the sake of your souls. Should I be the less loved, because I love you all the more?*

Not only will St. Paul care for his community like a father, he will do far more. He is ready to make all sacrifices, and finally to be offered up in sacrifice, on behalf of the church. He is not merely speaking of a general readiness to go to any lengths to help and finally to " sacrifice oneself." He uses terms and concepts taken from liturgical worship. In the same way he writes to the Philippians: " Even if I am to be poured out like a libation at the sacrifice and liturgy of your faith, I still rejoice and rejoice with all of you " (Phil. 2:17). When the church of Philippi offers sacrifice and liturgical worship its Apostle must be included among the offerers, indeed, among the sacrifices offered. St. Paul must be offered along with the oblation of the church. In this way he is mediator of grace, and his sacrifice will be for the salvation of souls. Thus he again affirms that the Apostle is not only a teacher. This he certainly is. But his service goes far wider and deeper. He is a priestly mediator between God and the church.

As he has already done at 11:11, St. Paul assures the Corin-

thians that he loves them more than all others do when he
refuses to be a burden on them for his support. His affirmation
takes the form of a reproachful question: Does this give them a
right to love him less?

[16]*Very well then, I made no heavy demands on you. But I was
perhaps very cunning and got hold of you by deceit?*

St. Paul answers a tacit objection. The Corinthians admit that
St. Paul himself was not a burden to them. But he has used
deceitful methods, and he puts his selfish plans into effect by
means of envoys. Perhaps this is what his opponents in Corinth
were saying, and he had already come to hear of their reproach.
Or perhaps he is simply forestalling such suspicions. He had in
fact organized a collection for Jerusalem at Corinth, and was
actually using envoys to see it through, as chapters 8 and 9 explain. He had already (8:20) expressed his fear of being criticized
for his handling of the large sums in question.

[17]*Did I use any of those whom I sent to you to overreach you?*

Grieved at the thought, St. Paul reminds his readers of how
unjust and absurd such suspicions would be. It is enough to put
some questions. The answers must be obvious to the Corinthians.
No proof will be needed. No one can seriously maintain that St.
Paul is trying to enrich himself by means of his envoys.

[18]*I asked Titus [to visit you] and sent brothers with him. Did
Titus perhaps overreach you? Have we ourselves not walked in
the same spirit? Have we not gone the same path?*

It is true that St. Paul had already sent Titus once to Corinth
(8:6) and was sending him again with some brothers (i.e. Chris-

tians), to take up the collection (8:16–18). But no one would accuse Titus of having made money for himself, and St. Paul may certainly associate himself with Titus. They are both inspired by the same spirit, and go the same way. Hence the Corinthians must ascribe to both the same innocence and the same honesty.

Anxieties of Paul about His Visit (12:19–21)

¹⁹*You have been thinking, no doubt, this long time that we are defending ourselves to you. We are speaking before God in Christ. But it is all for your edification.*

There are some misgivings and anxieties with regard to his visit which St. Paul wishes to speak of before coming to Corinth. First, there is a misunderstanding to be avoided. His letter might be taken wrongly. It is to a great extent the Apostle's speech in his own defense. But St. Paul is not trying to clear himself before the judgment seat of the Corinthians. He stands in the sight of God, and it is before God that he justifies himself. This letter, like everything else, is comprised within the new being in Christ. This guarantees the truth of what he writes, just as it guarantees his desire to serve in love. It is not a matter of his personal interests when the Apostle defends his office and his ministry. His one end and object after all is to build up the church.

²⁰*I was afraid that when I came I should not find you as I should wish you to be, and that you would not find me as you would wish me to be. There might have been strife, jealousies, anger,*

quarrels, denunciations, whispering campaigns, arrogance, and
disorders [*among you*].

The church of Corinth is urgently in need of being set in order
and strengthened. St. Paul was afraid that on his arrival he
would not find the church in the condition he desired. And he
was also afraid that he would have to reprimand and punish the
Corinthians, which would mean that they too would not find
Paul himself as they would like him to be. He lists a number of
gross faults and sins which he feared to find in the community.
It is not the only example of such a " catalog of vices " in the
New Testament. Such lists are, no doubt, often merely conventional, as may be seen from the fact that they have parallels outside the New Testament in pagan as well as Jewish writings.
We may not, therefore, at once conclude that the faults listed
were notoriously rife in the community in question. Here, however, all the sins spring from contention and animosity. And
we know from 1 Corinthians as well as 2 Corinthians that there
were rival parties, dissensions, and conflicts in the community.
Here, therefore, St. Paul means each word to apply to real conditions in the community, and takes them to task in the hope of
making them reflect and amend their behavior.

[21] [*I was afraid*] *that when I came to you again, my God would*
humble me before you, and that I should have to grieve over
many who have sinned and not done penance for the·impurity
and unchastity and licentiousness in which they have indulged.

Finally, there was the fear that his visit to Corinth would show
him that many who had sinned earlier had remained impeni-
tent. The sins in question are named in a new catalog of vices

as sins of immorality, especially of sexual license. In 1 Corinthians St. Paul had in fact been obliged to give reprimands and punishments for such sins (1 Cor. 5 : 1–11 on account of a case of gross immorality and 1 Cor. 6 : 12–20 on account of dealings with prostitutes). The city of Corinth had a bad reputation in antiquity on account of its loose morals. It is understandable, therefore, that even the Christian community should have been burdened by defects in sexual morality. St. Paul's rebukes may presuppose cases in which Christians brought with them into the church sins and sinful relationships from the time before their conversion and had still not mended their ways. Or he may be thinking of cases in which the sins were committed after entry into the church and the sinners had not found the strength to repent, as was understandable, after all, in the conditions then reigning at Corinth. The whole situation caused grave scandal in the church, and discredited it in the eyes of the outside world. One of the objects of St. Paul's visit must have been the conversion of such sinners.

But in the meantime, the very thought of such sins grieved the Apostle deeply. It is the grief of the pastor and educator at the faults of his charges, and anxious care for their eternal salvation. St. Paul feels the situation as a humiliation for himself. A flourishing church is the pride and joy of the Apostle, who in fact had said earlier that the church of Corinth was his pride (1 : 14) and his letter of recommendation (3 : 3) wherever he went. Abuses could only be a humiliation to him, since he was responsible for the community. Their defects reflect on him, as he had pointed out already: " Who is weak and I am not also weak? Where does anyone fall that I am not inflamed?" (11 : 29).

This humiliation is felt by St. Paul as inflicted by the hand of God. He sees in these painful experiences the disposition of God's sovereign rule over him, though no doubt in the sense that God wishes to purify his Apostle and draw him to himself in all things. Inspired by a sense of intimate union, the Apostle here, as on some other occasions, calls God " his God."

Paul's Warnings and Hopes (13:1–10)

^{13:1}*I am on my way to you now for the third time. " If two or three witnesses affirm it, the matter is established"* [*Deut. 19:15*].

St. Paul speaks warmly and urgently. His words are intimate and appealing. Once more (cf. 12:14) he announces his third visit. This visit has a special importance, and will be decisive for his relationship to the church of Corinth. He underlines the significance of its being his third visit by quoting a saying of scripture. Here he shows himself a true rabbinical scholar. According to Old Testament law, all issues brought before the courts were decided on the testimony of three witnesses. The three visits form the three witnesses who will determine the relationship between St. Paul and the church of Corinth. Hence the third visit is to silence all contradiction, settle all disputes, and restore definitive peace.

²*I have given warning already, and I give warning now, as I did personally on my second visit and now repeat by letter, speaking to the sinners and to all the rest, that when I come once more, I shall be ruthless.*

The warnings which St. Paul had given during his second visit will be carried out at his third. He will proceed ruthlessly against the offenders. He means, no doubt, those in particular who cause divisions and quarrels (12:20) and also those who have been guilty of sexual offenses (12:21). He will call them to account, and if they persist in disobedience, exclude them from the community.

³You are, after all, asking for proof that Christ speaks in me, he who is not weak in your regard but is strong among you.

St. Paul justifies his threat of ruthless action by saying that the Corinthians themselves desire it. They are asking for proof that Christ speaks with power in the Apostle. St. Paul finds that their demand is quite reasonable. And he will give the necessary proof to show that Christ truly speaks in him. Like every other Christian, St. Paul is " in Christ " (13:4). This short formula is used by St. Paul to describe the fellowship and union of Christians with Christ. Christ comprises and contains all things and all Christians. For he is the head of the church (Eph. 1:22; Col. 1:18), the beginning and sum-total of the new humanity (Rom. 5:15), the prototype and form of all creation (Col. 1:16). Hence St. Paul can say: " It is not I that live, but Christ lives in me " (Gal. 2:20), and " Christ must be formed in you " (Gal. 4:19). St. Paul can say: " We in Christ " (2:12.17 etc.), or again: " Christ in us " (13:3.5). Hence just as the Apostle speaks in Christ, so too Christ speaks in the Apostle.

This truth will be made manifest by St. Paul's authoritative intervention. The Apostle is well aware of his natural weakness, of which he has spoken often enough. But he also knows that in spite of his weakness, or rather, through this weakness, from beginning to end, Christ speaks and works in him. Feeble though the human being Paul may be, he will prove himself strong against the Corinthians. He will reveal himself in the signs, wonders, and mighty deeds (12:12) which accompany and support the ministry of the Apostle.

4He was crucified in his weakness, but he lives by the power of God. So too we are surely weak in him, but we shall live with him by the power of God against you.

The Apostle is like his Lord Christ in weakness and in strength. Christ too was weak when he was crucified. But then he was raised up and glorified by the power of God, and now he lives and reigns in power as the exalted Lord. The Apostle is in Christ. To be in Christ means to be weak with him and to share his passion and death. But it also means that the Apostle participates, by God's gift, in the life and power of the exalted Lord. This life it not merely the future life, which only comes in eternity. It is already a mighty force in the Apostle, and will be powerful in him when he appears shortly in Corinth.

The weakness and power of Christ are often mentioned together in the New Testament, as opposites which complement one another. It is no doubt an ancient formula, which was fixed before St. Paul wrote. It is a brief, ancient *Credo* by which faith and preaching overcame the scandal of the cross. The cross could never have preached alone. It would have been only the story of a dreadful end. It must always have been linked to the message of the resurrection, which revealed the cross as the way of passing into life.

5Put yourselves to the test to see that you are living in the faith, to see where you stand! Or do you not recognize yourselves as such that Jesus Christ is in you? You would have had to fail the test!

Verses 5–10 form a connected group of thoughts in which St. Paul urges the community to put itself to the test, so that its faith and life may be genuine, and the Apostle be spared the unhappiness of having to condemn and punish when he comes. Instead of wishing to have proof that Christ works in the Apostle (13:3), the Corinthians would do better to put themselves to the proof. The community knows of the reality of Christ in the church. It knows that Christians are in Christ just as Christ is in Christians (13:3). This is a reality which the Corinthians must not forget, but must try to make effective in a life inspired by faith. The only true faith is that which is lived out in real life and action. If they did not know this and did not live up to it, they would have been tried and found wanting. And St. Paul would have to fear that they would also fail the test in the coming judgment.

⁶But I hope that you will recognize that we have not failed the test.

As he ponders anxiously the state of the community, the Apostle thinks once more of the struggle he must carry on for his office. So he inserts a brief remark. His mention of the community makes him express his confidence that they will at least recognize the Apostle's quality, even though they must admit their own defects.

⁷We pray God that you may do nothing bad at all, not so that we may appear well qualified, but so that you may do right, even though we may seem to have failed the test.

St. Paul corrects himself at once. It is not important that he should be shown to be tried and true (13:6). What is all-important is that the community avoid all evil and be steadfast in good, and hence pass the test. This is the Apostle's prayer. If it is answered, he will in fact lose the opportunity of displaying his power in Corinth, and his good alloy will not then be demonstrated. But he gladly renounces such a chance of proving his worth, for the sake of the Corinthians.

⁸For we have no power against the truth, but only for it.

It does not matter what happens to St. Paul personally, provided the truth triumphs. The word " truth " is to be taken in its biblical sense. We think of truth as a right statement and hence as something in the realm of our thought. In the Bible, truth is a valid and right reality, and hence something in the realm of subsistence. In this sense the truth is in God, since the right and true reality of all things is comprised in him. In God's revelation in the world the truth is made manifest and present in the world. Hence Jesus can say in the Gospel of St. John that he is " the way, the truth, and the life " (Jn. 14:6). From this point of view the right order of things is the truth. St. Paul has the right order of things at heart, that is, the right relationship between God and the world, the right relationship of the church to God, and the right order in the church itself. It means faith, peace, the moral constancy of the church. His one object, which causes him all his unrest and all his toil, is to manifest and build up this truth in his apostolic preaching.

⁹We rejoice when we are weak but you are strong. And this is what we pray for—your perfect well-being.

For the sake of the truth, St. Paul can only be glad if the church in Corinth is strong, even though he appears as the weak one.

The shape of things must be what he has already said: " Thus death works in us, but life in you " (4 : 12). And hence he prays for this. He is ready to be delivered up as a sacrifice for the community (12 : 15). Everything must serve to build up and perfect the church.

[10]*Hence I write so while I am away, so that when I am present I may not have to be stern in the use of the authority which the Lord gave me in order to build up and not to pull down.*

The building up of the church was also the purpose of St. Paul's letter. He hopes that the effect will be to remove all grounds for taking stern action when he himself comes in the near future. He does not fail to emphasize that the apostolic authority given him by the Lord also empowers him to take strict measures when necessary. But the ultimate goal can never be punitive destruction, but only the building up of the church.

THE CLOSING OF THE LETTER
(13:11-13)

GREETINGS AND GOOD WISHES (13:11–13)

¹¹For the rest, brothers, rejoice, let yourselves be perfected, give heed to our exhortation, be of one mind, be peaceable, and the God of love and peace will be with you.

The final greeting contains some words and formulas which are part of the conventional style in ending a letter. But the greeting as a whole and in its details is still oriented to the particular conditions of the church at Corinth. " Rejoice " could simply be the usual wish of the end of a letter. But St. Paul very often attaches a deeper meaning to the word. At the beginning of the letter he called the apostles " servants of [the divinely-inspired] joy " (1:24). Joy is " joy in Christ " (Phil. 3:1), which comes from " being in Christ." Hence it is essential to the condition of the Christian. It is an effect and an expression of the salvation bestowed upon the church. When St. Paul wishes joy, he wishes the gift of salvation.

The conventional greetings also include the wishing of peace. But in the present letter, this greeting has a special purpose and weight. It is embodied in a number of words of similar import, and is aimed at the partitions, strife, and dissensions of the Corinthian community. The greeting is confirmed by the promise that the God of peace dwells with the peaceable.

¹²Greet one another with the holy kiss. All the saints send you their greetings.

213

The newly-found harmony of the community is to be sealed with the " holy kiss," the " kiss of peace." This was not just a figurative formula. The brotherly kiss was really exchanged. The custom must have been practiced during the assemblies which brought the community together, the kiss being an assurance of their mutual fellowship. Possibly the sermon which was part of the primitive Christian liturgy ended with the call for the kiss of peace. When the community had received a letter from an apostle, it would certainly have been read instead of the sermon. Here the letter ends, as the sermon ordinarily did, with the summons to exchange the kiss, which would mean not only fellowship and peace among the hearers, but also with the absent Apostle. Just as the preacher was normally the first to give the kiss, as he summoned the faithful to give this sign to each other, so that the kiss was passed on from him around the church, so too St. Paul uses the letter to impart the kiss of peace to the church and accepts it from the faithful. In this way the link between the Apostle and the community is also restored.

Having given his own greetings, St. Paul adds greetings from all the saints, that is, from all the Christians who were about St. Paul as he wrote the letter.

[13]*The grace of the Lord Jesus Christ and the love of God and the fellowship of the Holy Spirit be with you all.*

The blessing called down upon the Corinthians is very rich in meaning. The Apostle mentions Christ, God, and Spirit in close connection, while still distinguishing them, since he assigns the blessing in question to each in particular: grace proceeding from Christ, love from the Father, and the bond of union from the

Holy Spirit. The solemn tone reminds us at once of the prayers with which we now adore the Holy Trinity.

In other places the formula used by St. Paul has only one member (Rom. 16:20: " The grace of our Lord Jesus Christ be with you ") or only two (1 Cor. 8:6: "One God, the Father, from whom comes everything . . . and one Lord, Jesus Christ, through whom comes everything "). The expressions can develop into a three-membered formula as here at 13:13. We have already noted in 1:21f. and 3:3 the sequence Father, Son, Spirit. Another three-membered formula is given at Romans 15:30: " I appeal to you, my brothers, through our Lord Jesus Christ and the love of the Spirit, to strive along with me in your prayers to God." Other complete three-membered formulas are to be found at Matthew 3:16f.; 28:19; 1 Corinthians 12:4-6; Ephesians 4:4-6; 1 Peter 1:2.

The fuller three-membered formulas arose gradually in the New Testament, being developed from the simpler forms. The sequence in which the names appear is far from being as fixed as it is today. It changes with the context. Here the sequence Christ, God, Holy Spirit is to be explained as follows. The first direct gift to Christians is the grace of Jesus Christ. It sanctifies from sin and thus gives access to the Father (Rom. 5:1). The fellowship of the Holy Spirit, that is, the fellowship brought about by the Holy Spirit and subsisting in him, embraces and fills all things (1 Cor. 12:11). The sequence with which we are familiar appears in the New Testament in the command to baptize: " Baptize in the name of the Father and of the Son and of the Holy Spirit " (Mt. 28:19). Such phrases are the New Testament foundation of the doctrine of the Holy Trinity which was later given such a rich development in the church.

CONCLUSION

2 Corinthians is a controversial fighting letter. St. Paul is giving battle for his community. Did the letter succeed in achieving its goals? Did St. Paul succeed in restoring peace and union with his church at Corinth?

He says in 10:15 that he intends to use Corinth as his base for further missions once the church is firmly established at Corinth. In his letter to the Romans, written about a year later at Corinth, he says that his plan now is to go to Rome next and after a short stay there go on to Spain to preach the gospel. An ancient tradition of the Roman church, which can be traced back as far as the first century, affirms that St. Paul succeeded in carrying out this plan. Hence the condition which he laid down in 10:15f. must have been verified. Confidence had been restored between himself and the Corinthians, and he could then pursue his further plans for his missions.

In 2 Corinthians, St. Paul makes a fierce onslaught on certain missionaries whom he brands as pseudo-apostles and as intruders in his mission field. Was it necessary to give battle? St. Paul always begins his letters by wishing his readers grace and peace. It is his profound desire that the God of peace should conquer the spirit of discord in the church (Rom. 16:20). One of the most beautiful passages in all his letters is the " Canticle of Love " (1 Cor. 13). And in 2 Corinthians itself St. Paul is striving for fellowship and peace with the community in Corinth. Nonetheless, he considered that the hard and wearing struggle was necessary for the sake of the truth of the gospel, and for the purity and authenticity of doctrine and faith (11:4). In the following centuries the church often had to give battle for the sake of the true faith. The church has often been reproached for intolerance. But it was convinced, as it still is convinced, that this struggle had and has to be waged for the truth of the gospel.

But the state of affairs revealed by the New Testament in this connection is in some ways disheartening. All the letters of St. Paul, like the other Catholic Letters in the New Testament, tell us of controversies and struggles. Other writings of the New Testament allude to their existence. Sometimes the conflict was concerned with the purity of doctrine and the proper conduct of life, but often enough it was also based on personal animosities in the communities. The communities were barely twenty or thirty years old, and the church was already torn and divided by contradictions. Was the *one* church ever realized? Or was it never anything but the lofty ideal for which desire and faith longed and still long?